STRESS TEST:
HOW DONALD TRUMP
THREATENS AMERICAN
DEMOCRACY

STRESS TEST:
HOW DONALD TRUMP
THREATENS AMERICAN
DEMOCRACY
WILLIAM COOPER

THE **BLACK SPRING**
PRESS GROUP

PRAISE FOR WILLIAM COOPER AND STRESS TEST

"*Stress Test* is a compelling rallying cry for democratic institutions under threat in America."

—*Publishers Weekly*

"A compelling and sensible overview of America's emerging democratic crisis … the book's reasoned tone and bipartisan critiques are a welcome perspective in an increasingly polarized and heated political landscape."

—*Kirkus Reviews*

"An excellent short historical and predictive account of where America stands today and how recent history will inform its future."

—*Manhattan Book Review*

"William Cooper's collection of columns is essential reading for anyone who cares about the future of our democracy."

—*Reader's Favorite (Five-Star Review)*

"William Cooper is an insightful and thought-provoking writer about us politics. He deserves to be widely read."

—*Thomas Plate, bestselling author of Conversations With Lee Kuan Yew, Oped Columnist, South China Morning Post*

"William Cooper is a leading global commentator on us politics."

—*Channel News Asia*

"William Cooper's...editorials are always thought-provoking and spark much-needed political discussion."

—*Lindsey Chastain, Editor-in-Chief, Skiatook Journal*

"William Cooper is a welcome splash of reality on money, law and politics."

—*Tennessee Tribune*

"United States journalist William Cooper provides keen insights about America's constitutional democracy."

—*Modern Ghana*

"William Cooper is a very insightful and pertinent author about world affairs."

—*The City Paper Bogotá*

First published in 2022
An Eyewear Publishing book, The Black Spring Press Group
Grantully Road, Maida Vale, London w9
United Kingdom

Typeset User Design, Illustration and Typesetting, UK
Cover art Zeljka Kojic

The author has requested the publisher use American
spelling and grammar wherever possible in this edition

ISBN-13 978-1-913606-68-8

To my family.

TABLE OF CONTENTS

ABOUT THE AUTHOR

William Cooper is an attorney and columnist. His writings have appeared in over one hundred publications globally including *The New York Times*, *Wall Street Journal*, *New York Daily News*, *San Francisco Chronicle*, *Baltimore Sun*, *USA Today*, *Chicago Sun-Times*, *Jerusalem Post*, and *Huffington Post*.

"There are few things wholly evil or wholly good. Almost everything, especially of government policy, is an inseparable compound of the two, so that our best judgment of the preponderance between them is continually demanded."

—*Abraham Lincoln*

"The truth unquestionably is, that the only path to a subversion of the republican system of the Country is, by flattering the prejudices of the people, and exciting their jealousies and apprehensions, to throw affairs into confusion, and bring on civil commotion."

—*Alexander Hamilton*

INTRODUCTION

T his book is a collection of my previously published columns about American democracy. The columns explain how a frenzy of misbehavior and misjudgment threatens the American polity.

Donald Trump is the center of the storm. His words, deeds and basic instincts are fundamentally at odds with America's long-held essential ideals. But Trump isn't the only problem. Many of his friends, and plenty of his foes, also consistently violate important norms and traditions while seeking short-term political victories. This bipartisan race to the bottom is a stress test of the world's preeminent constitutional democracy.

It continues today.

The columns in this book detail how Trump-era politics test four essential (and overlapping) principles of American democracy. The first is fidelity to the Constitution of the United States. Throughout American history government officials have broadly respected, honored, and followed the Constitution. Yet Donald Trump, the 45th President of the United States, neither understands nor respects the Constitution. He has called the document "a foreign language," disparaged the Emoluments Clause as "the phony Emoluments Clause," and claimed that "I have an Article 2 where I have the right to do whatever I want as president." Many in Trump's Republican party have encouraged and supported Trump's anti-constitutional behavior. And many

Democrats, too, have cast aside long-held constitutional traditions in their frenetic effort to oppose Trump.

The second essential principle of American democracy tested during the Trump era is respect for the rule of law. The law must be applied evenly to all people. Always. Since Trump's ascendancy in 2015, however, one's political affiliation has often mattered more than the underlying facts relating to one's guilt or innocence. Trump has been the worst offender of all, consistently calling for prosecutions of his political opponents—including Hillary Clinton, Barack Obama and Joe Biden. But both sides of the aisle have criminalized American politics. Democratic Speaker of the House Nancy Pelosi, for example, said about Trump in June of 2019: "I don't want to see him impeached. I want to see him in prison." In a healthy democracy politicians focus their attention on the ballot box—not the jailhouse. And America's descent towards the criminalized politics of failed states is a disturbing symptom of the nation's broader affliction.

The third essential principle of American democracy tested during this time is the commitment to rational government. American democracy has lasted for centuries not simply because of the words in the Constitution. It has succeeded because of a national ethos firmly rooted in rationality, as embodied by America's founders. While there have certainly been exceptions, reason and prudence have long shaped American public policy.

With Trump atop the Republican party, however, American politics have descended into a whirlpool of lies, false narratives and abhorrent stupidities. This irrationality has enveloped not just the populace but elected officials across the political aisle. The insanity of the fringe has risen to and infected the highest levels of American government.

The result has been a steady procession of public policy failures. The most shocking failure was the election of a constitutionally illiterate reality-television personality as president. But Trump's presidency is only one example of a broader problem. America has nearly defaulted on its debts; millions of Americans have opposed simple health measures to fight the coronavirus; tens of thousands have died annually from drug overdoses; the federal deficit has exploded while basic infrastructure has gone into disrepair; state legislatures have fixated on distorting and limiting the franchise; economic inequality has increased exponentially; and the existential threat to the environment has gone largely unaddressed.

A rational polity would not let any, let alone all, of these sweeping policy failures occur.

Finally, perhaps the most important principle of American government challenged since Trump took office is the very notion that government officials are chosen by the people in free and fair elections. This premise of democracy has defined America from its outset. Yet Donald Trump and many of his Republican allies have attacked it, openly and unapologetically. Trump's behavior leading up to, during, and after the 2020 presidential election—promulgating the "Big Lie" that he, not Joe Biden, actually won the election—is the most destructive behavior of any president (or former president) in American history. Even after Trump's supporters' shocking riot at the United States Capitol on January 6, 2021, the "Big Lie" continues on as the central Republican platform heading into the 2022 congressional elections. Throughout the country Republicans in state office are reengineering their election systems so their future attempts to thwart voters' intentions are more likely to succeed.

These violations of American democracy's core principles are stunning. Yet, at the same time, many Americans have acted admirably in the Trump age. The Judiciary, for example, has largely remained a rational branch of government. Its wholesale rejection of Trump's postelection litigation claims was both expected and reassuring. Governmental officials on both sides of the aisle, moreover, continue to uniformly respect and follow court orders. Moderate senators with responsible objectives continue to exert important influence in both political parties. And, ultimately, there was a timely transfer of power after Joe Biden's inauguration in January 2021: Trump went home when his term ended.

Battered and bruised, American democracy withstood the Trump presidency.

Like all stress tests, the American stress test reveals its subject's strengths and its weaknesses. American democracy has proven to be both sturdy and vulnerable. The key to the future is the same overriding variable that has shaped the past: Donald Trump. The longer he dominates the Republican party the more likely America ultimately fails the stress test and descends into a lesser form of government.

And Trump is, still, the most popular Republican in the country. By a mile.

The columns in this book begin in 2019, after the Democrats won a majority in the House of Representatives.

They continue, in chronological order, through the first few months of 2022, nearly 15 months into Joe Biden's presidency. As they detail, the American stress test shows few signs of abating.

1/   IMPEACHMENT 1.0

"An impeachable offense is whatever a majority of the House of Representatives considers it to be at a given moment in history."

—*Gerald R. Ford*

THE columns in this chapter cover the Democrats' first impeachment of Donald Trump. But to understand what motivated the Democrats' 2019 effort to remove Trump from office, one must first understand what Trump had been up to the previous eight years.

His political ascension began with a lie. Starting in 2011, Trump claimed that then-president Barack Obama was born in Kenya and therefore couldn't be president under the Constitution: "I have people that have been studying [Obama's birth certificate] and they cannot believe what they're finding" Trump said. "I would like to have him show his birth certificate, and can I be honest with you, I hope he can. Because if he can't, if he can't, if he wasn't born in this country, which is a real possibility … then he has pulled one of the great cons in the history of politics."

At the time this demagoguery was easily dismissed as the despicable (yet inconsequential) machinations of a low-grade propagandist. Few took Trump seriously. In retrospect, however, the "birther" lie was a fitting prelude to Trump's political rise. It was baseless, shameless, inflammatory—and stunningly effective. Among the many unfortunate lessons we have learned from Trump is not just that lying works politically, but that blatant falsehoods resonate with large swathes of the electorate if they're consistent with already simmering prejudices.

Trump announced his campaign for president in June of 2015. It was met with dismissiveness, even laughter, within established political circles. As Chris Cilliza wrote in the Washington Post, Trump's "announcement was greeted with something between incredulity (Trump has flirted with running many times before) and amazement (Trump is Trump). The prevailing sentiment seemed to be a collective eye roll and a laugh." Cilliza then categorically asserted the then-prevailing view: "Donald Trump will never be president. He knows that. We know that."

Trump's campaign focused relentlessly on inflaming the basest parts of American society. It mixed toxic politics—sharp division, open xenophobia, myopic nationalism—with the crown jewel of American public relations: celebrity scandal. Trump promised to ban Muslims from entering the United States and to build a wall at the Southern border with Mexico. About the latter, he said: "I would build a great wall, and nobody builds walls better than me, believe me, and I'll build them very inexpensively. I will build a great great wall on our southern border and I'll have Mexico pay for that wall."

During the Republican Primaries Trump levied personal insults against his opponents Jeb Bush, Marco Rubio, and Ted Cruz (targeting their personalities, physical characteristics, and family members). He did not even pretend to possess two key ingredients of traditional political success: character and decency.

And it worked. Trump won the Republican nomination.

Next came the general election against Democratic nominee Hillary Clinton. The establishment consensus that he would lose remained strong. "Donald Trump is not going to be President of the United States," Nancy Pelosi said after Trump secured the nomination. "Take it to the bank, I guarantee it."

In the general election, Trump's dirty politics got

dirtier: He zeroed in on Hillary's unauthorized use of private email as Secretary of State (saying she should go to jail) and Bill Clinton's sex life (obsessing over the former president's real and imagined indiscretions). And Trump got help. The Russians hacked the Democratic National Committee and dumped embarrassing emails online. And FBI Director James Comey announced, 11 days before the election, that the FBI was investigating Hillary for her email practices.

Trump won. A reality-television star with no government experience who ran on a cartoonish platform—long on hatred and short on reason—joined George Washington, Abraham Lincoln, and Franklin Delano Roosevelt as one of 45 people to ever hold the United States presidency. As *The New York Times* put it, Trump's "surprise victory ended an erratic and grievance-filled campaign that took direct aim at his own party and long-held ideals of American democracy."

Surrounded by a crew of inexperienced and controversial misfits (including Chief of Staff Reince Priebus, National Security Adviser Michael Flynn, and Senior Counselor Steve Bannon) Trump plunged into the presidency headfirst—and blind. He immediately issued the clumsy, blatantly unconstitutional Executive Order 13769 (the "Travel Ban"), seeking to block millions of Muslims from entering the country. As Benjamin Wittes wrote on Lawfare, "the malevolence of President Trump's Executive Order on visas and refugees is mitigated chiefly—and perhaps only—by the astonishing incompetence of its drafting and construction." After widespread public outrage and internal protest at the Department of Justice—culminating in Trump firing Acting Attorney General Sally Yates—Trump abruptly replaced the Travel Ban with a still-clumsy, watered-down version.

And it was downhill from there.

By the time the Democrats assumed a majority in the House of Representatives in 2019 Trump had—from the Oval Office—denigrated the Constitution, undermined the rule of law, and abandoned rational governance in favor of his own brand of dysfunctional, me-first misman-agement. After trying to ban Muslims from entering the country, Trump threatened nuclear war with North Korea; cycled through numerous senior advisers and cabinet offi-cials; detained thousands of migrant families at the border; took the word of Russian president Vladimir Putin over his own intelligence community; battled with the Department of Justice; demeaned America's allies; and equated violent white supremacists with peaceful protesters.

He did all of this while being cheered on wildly by tens of millions of his supporters and firmly protected by Republicans controlling both chambers of Congress.

It was understandable, then, that—after all Trump had done to test American democracy—the Democrats were highly motivated to oppose Trump when they took the House.

But they overreached.

How to respond to a Donald Trump presidency is, of course, not an easy question. The optimal approach would have been to robustly oppose Trump while, at the same time, doubling down on American democracy's essential princi-ples. This would have strengthened American democracy by setting the right precedent for the future and showing that America's norms and traditions work under pressure.

They do.

All too often, however, the Democrats' cast them aside. Instead of rising above Trump, they got in the mud with him. While accusing Trump of lying, they lied themselves. While accusing Trump of shattering norms, they shattered norms, too. While accusing Trump of casting aside long-term considerations in pursuit of short-term political interests, they did so themselves. And they were joined, hand in hand, by tens of millions of Americans and a fiercely anti-Trump mainstream press.

One example of this overreaction was the process surrounding Trump's first impeachment. The Constitution allows Congress to impeach and remove a sitting president for "treason, bribery, or other high crimes or misdemeanors." This is a high standard; as it must be. The American people all vote on the same question on only one occasion: the presidential election. Lowering the standard of impeachment and removal too far would thus result in a direct corresponding infringement of the people's will—the core basis of governmental legitimacy.

The Democrats didn't care. They were openly searching for a basis to impeach Trump from the moment he won the 2016 presidential election. When Trump pressured Ukrainian President Volodymyr Zelenskiy to investigate the Bidens, the Democrats had their hook. And off they went.

The columns that follow tell the story.

JULY 31, 2019
THE CURRENT IMPEACHMENT CALCULUS

THE list of Democrats who favor initiating formal impeachment proceedings against President Trump continues to grow. And the strong urge to remove the most divisive and incompetent president in modern times is understandable. Until recently, all the Democrats could do was sit and watch as Trump's dizzying mismanagement of the executive branch was protected by Republican majorities in both chambers of Congress. With a majority in the House firmly in hand, the Democrats are now looking for any opportunity to remove Trump from office.

This is a mistake. The way to counteract Donald Trump's belligerence is to fiercely oppose him while respecting America's core traditions and institutions. Impeachment should be reserved only for clear examples of "treason, bribery, or other high crimes or misdemeanors" under the United States Constitution. While Trump's behavior with respect to Special Counsel Robert Mueller's investigation was grossly improper, it does not rise to this level.

First, Article 2 of the Constitution vests the executive power solely in the president: "The executive power shall be vested in a President of the United States." There is a legitimate debate at the Supreme Court and in the legal academy, therefore, regarding whether a special counsel—a creature of the executive branch—is constitutionally permitted to investigate the president in the first place.

Second, Trump did cooperate in meaningful ways with

Mueller's investigation, choosing not to assert privilege while providing Mueller's team millions of pages of relevant documents and making numerous senior officials available for lengthy interviews. He didn't have to. And of course Trump did not fire Mueller nor shut down the investigation—as he could have.

Finally, Trump's anger towards Mueller must be considered in context. Mueller did not find that Trump's campaign colluded with Russia to hack into the Democratic National Committee's email servers in 2016. And the evidence suggesting Trump's campaign did so was always sparse. The duly elected President of the United States is not required to sit by meekly as unelected prosecutors within the executive branch zealously investigate him for something he didn't do. Even Donald Trump has constitutional prerogatives.

Again—this is not to say that Trump's behavior was proper. It wasn't. But the question at hand is whether he should be the first United States President removed from office. Ever. As Democratic Speaker of the House Nancy Pelosi—who is pushing back on calls to initiate impeachment proceedings—understands, the answer is no. "I'm not for impeachment," Pelosi said in March 2019. "Impeachment is so divisive to the country that unless there's something so compelling and overwhelming *and bipartisan*, I don't think we should go down that path, because it divides the country," she said. (Emphasis added.) "He's just not worth it."

This is still true today. Trump's not worth it. Overreaching with a partisan impeachment would set a dangerous precedent, one Republicans in Congress would undoubtedly weaponize in the future.

Indeed, as the Mueller report grows older—and the presidential election draws nearer—the political calculus is clear: The net impact of pursuing impeachment would favor Trump, not his opponents.

For starters, a partisan impeachment effort would energize Trump's base. In stark contrast to the Nixon impeachment proceedings (which commenced with a bipartisan House vote of 410 to 4) this battle would be fought sharply along party lines.

Impeachment would thus solidify Trump's core supporters' conviction that liberal Washington elites (the "Deep State") are unfairly targeting him. An iron law of American politics is that the more Trump's opposition attacks him outside of the rules the more frenetically his base supports him.

Conducting impeachment proceedings—on top of the historically robust ongoing congressional investigations into Trump—would, moreover, offend more-moderate Trump supporters. They want Congress to focus on passing quality legislation. America suffers from stunning public-policy failures including deteriorating infrastructure, exploding economic inequality and dangerous climate change. Ignoring these matters and fixating on removing Trump from office prematurely is counterproductive. Bill Clinton's approval ratings improved during his impeachment proceedings, largely driven by the disgust of moderate Americans who found the Republicans' behavior a bitter diversion from what mattered. Democrats should try to attract moderate voters, not repel them, as the presidential election approaches.

These concerns counsel against impeachment even in light of the Clinton impeachment, a reckless Republican overreach. As historian Robert Dallek explained, "Clinton's egregious act of self-indulgence was outdone by an impeachment based not on constitutionally required high crimes and misdemeanors but on a vindictive determination to bring down a president who had offended self-righteous moralists eager to put a different political agenda in place." The Republicans' mistake then should not be used as justification for Democrats to make one now. Such Trumpian logic—that two wrongs do in fact make a right—should be rejected, even if the target is Trump himself.

Perhaps it would, ultimately, be worth both energizing Trump supporters and setting bad precedent if impeachment proceedings carried a proportionate offsetting gain. But they don't. Impeachment proceedings won't oust Trump. The Republican-controlled Senate will not convict him. (Who knows: Mitch McConnell might not even authorize a Senate trial if Trump is impeached by the House. He is, after all, the same guy who refused to hold confirmation hearings for President Obama's Supreme Court nominee Merrick Garland.)

Impeachment would thus be, at best, a cathartic victory for a subset of Democrats. At worst, it would be the energizing catalyst to reelect Trump. Either way, pursuing impeachment would likely be a net negative, perhaps making a statement that Trump's behavior was unacceptable but galvanizing his supporters—as they march towards the ballot box—in the process.

Importantly, however, if facts emerge that Trump actually has committed a constitutional high crime then of course impeachment is appropriate. The key is this: Trump must actually *commit* an impeachable offense. A sitting president should not be impeached based on the overreaching allegations and nervous imaginations of his political rivals. America has constitutional rules and norms. They should be followed, not rewritten, when contemplating whether to impeach a duly elected president.

Even Donald Trump.

OCTOBER 23, 2019
DON'T OVERREACH IN QUEST TO IMPEACH

IMPEACHMENT's complicated.

On the one hand, Donald Trump pressured a foreign leader to investigate a political rival, setting off serious alarm bells regarding abuse of power. On the other, impeachment is an extraordinary constitutional remedy intended only for the gravest circumstances.

A successful impeachment would remove a president elected by the American people, the ultimate source of legitimacy in American democracy. The fundamental challenges to America's constitutional democracy experienced since Trump was elected president—and there have been many— would only compound if Democrats abuse Congress's impeachment power.

So how, then, should the Democrats approach impeaching Trump? First, the process must be fair both in appearance and substance. Ideally, an impeachment proceeding would be bipartisan. The alleged offense would be so clearly a crime—like Nixon ordering subordinates to commit burglary by breaking into the Democratic National Committee headquarters—that both sides would be unified in the effort.

That is not the case here. This is a partisan fight. The Democrats must therefore take every precaution to be fair and just. Any alternative would provide Trump helpful arguments in concurrent court proceedings and alienate large swaths of the electorate (many of whom are potential swing voters in next year's presidential election). Given that over a dozen Republican Senators must cross the aisle for Trump to be removed from office—a steep uphill battle—public opinion is paramount.

Second, impeachment should be based on a clear violation of an existing crime. The Constitution allows for impeachment only for "treason, bribery, or other high crimes and misdemeanors." While there's some ambiguity about what this means, and political calculations rightly play a role in the analysis, Congress should conscientiously respect the basic principles of criminal law given the gravity of the proceedings.

Trump is, indeed, neither above the law (as he sometimes thinks he is) nor below it (as some want him to be).

First among the fundamental principles of criminal law is that an unambiguous law must be on the books at the time of the alleged offense. As the rule of lenity sets forth, any ambiguity regarding the scope of the law must be resolved in favor of the defendant. This is not some random legal technicality. This is a bedrock principle of Anglo-American law rooted in rationality and fundamental fairness.

While the analysis will change as the investigation unfolds, current attempts to use campaign-finance regulations as a basis for establishing constitutional high crimes are strained and should be discarded. Trump should only be impeached if he committed a well-understood impeachable offense.

Finally, the Democrats must remember that they are writing a rule book that will eventually apply to them, too. Every step the Democrats take to remove Trump from office can—and perhaps likely will—be used against them in the future. If a Democrat is elected president in 2020, congressional Republicans will be salivating at the prospect of impeachment. The more the Democrats push the limits now, the less ability they would have, then, to resist impeachment.

Impeaching the president of the United States is not easy. Nor should it be. The founders recognized this by requiring a two-thirds majority in the Senate in order to convict. If the Democrats overreach and ignore these guideposts, their impeachment effort could boomerang into a net negative. It could even tip the scales toward Trump in 2020.

NOVEMBER 27, 2019
DEMOCRATS AND REPUBLICANS MUST SEPARATE
THE SIGNAL FROM THE NOISE

WHEN it comes to impeachment, both Democrats and Republicans need to narrow their focus. Two questions matter regarding impeachment. The first is factual: Did President Trump condition Ukraine's aid on an investigation into the Bidens? The second is legal: Would this quid pro quo constitute an impeachable offense?

Everything else is noise.

In Congress and much of the media, however, the noise is drowning out the signal. The impeachment proceedings have included lots of superfluous fanfare—from both sides of the aisle—that doesn't bear on the questions at hand. As Congress moves toward the momentous vote, it should home in on what matters and discard three attention-grabbing subjects from the impeachment analysis.

First, the Republicans should stop fixating on the identity of the whistleblower. The whistleblower report triggered the impeachment inquiry, but the Democrats' arguments do not depend on the report's author or its substance. There is ample independent evidence supporting allegations of a quid pro quo, including the Trump administration's public statements, the transcript of Trump's July 25, 2019 call with Ukrainian President Volodymyr Zelensky, and the testimony of numerous witnesses.

The identity of the whistleblower, moreover, is not relevant to any of Trump's potential defenses. The whistleblower had nothing to do with the events underlying the Democrats' allegations. The whistleblower simply kickstarted an investigation into them. As long as the evidence Democrats put forth independently establishes an impeachable offense, impeachment would be justified even if the whistleblower's identity is not revealed.

Second, the Democrats should stop focusing on Trump's firing of Ambassador Yovanovitch. Trump's removal of the ambassador may have been wrong-headed and handled improperly. But it was not a high crime or misdemeanor under the Constitution. A president does not commit an impeachable offense simply by disagreeing with, mistreating, or firing diplomats. To the extent there is a factual connection between Yovanovitch's removal and the pertinent question—whether Trump ordered a quid pro quo—then that linkage would be relevant.

To date, no such connection has been revealed. Indeed, Trump's replacement for Yovanovitch, Ambassador William Taylor, was vehemently opposed to any quid pro quo—undercutting the notion that replacing Yovanovitch with Taylor advanced the alleged scheme.

Finally, both sides should stop obsessing over Crowdstrike and whether the American cybersecurity company helped Ukraine interfere with the 2016 election. Trump's request for Ukraine to look into Crowdstrike may have been baseless, but it is not impeachable—even if it was a condition for Ukraine to receive the aid. Placing conditions on the distribution of foreign aid is commonplace. Conditioning aid on investigating a political rival may be impeachable; doing so for investigating flimsy allegations is not.

America's three-branch constitutional system would fundamentally weaken if legislators from the opposing party could review presidential communications with foreign leaders and shoehorn what they believed to be imprudent or baseless requests into impeachable offenses. As long as Trump did not cross any grave constitutional lines, he had wide latitude to request things from President Zelensky. For those shocked by Trump's Crowdstrike request, the remedy is the ballot box, not the Impeachment Clause.

Questions relating to the whistleblower, Ms. Yovanovitch, and Crowdstrike are, indeed, fundamentally important. They should be thoroughly investigated by Congress and the press, especially with the presidential election fast approaching. But they are outside the scope of the impeachment analysis.

What matters for impeachment is whether Trump conditioned aid on Ukraine investigating the Bidens and whether this constitutes an impeachable offense.

The rest is noise.

JANUARY 2, 2020
STATE OF DENIAL IN CONGRESS

SENATOR Susan Collins of Maine stated this week that it is "inappropriate, in my judgment, for senators on either side of the aisle to prejudge the evidence before they have heard what is presented to us, because each of us will take an oath, an oath that I take very seriously to render impartial justice."

She's spot on. So far, though, Congress has been anything but impartial when it comes to impeachment. Indeed, both the Democrats and Republicans have been in a hyper-partisan state of denial.

The question before Congress is whether to remove a sitting president. If they get this wrong it would set a precedent that could derail the presidency's essential position in America's constitutional constellation. From the beginning, our elected representatives should have developed the facts and analyzed the law with the uniform goal of getting this right. They have, instead, simply ignored anything inconsistent with predetermined party-line narratives.

The Democrats, for their part, cannot accept that Joe and Hunter Bidens' connections to Burisma (a Ukrainian oil company) matter. While there's no evidence that either Biden engaged in corruption or committed malfeasance, Joe's conflict of interest, itself, meets the very low threshold for being relevant to Trump's defense. While Vice President of the United States—a constitutional officer—Joe Biden withheld a billion dollars in congressionally authorized aid from Ukraine unless it fired a prosecutor who had investigated his son's company.

Sorry Democrats: This is not nothing.

While this conflict doesn't make Trump's acts proper, it is at least material to the question of whether he should be the first President—ever—removed from office. The Democrats have proclaimed, day after day, that Trump was using his office to "dig up dirt" on a "political rival." But the political rival was the previous Vice President, who was running the United States' Ukrainian policy. And the dirt related to a conflict of interest in existence when that political rival withheld a billion dollars of taxpayer money from Ukraine. This is different from Trump conditioning aid on Ukraine investigating Bernie Sanders' finances or spying on Elizabeth Warren's campaign.

Democrats nonetheless uniformly ignore the fact that Trump's pressuring of Ukraine did not happen on a blank slate. Setting aside whether the Democrats' conclusion (that Trump should be removed from office) is correct, there is a gaping void in their analysis. Put simply: In order to determine whether Trump's actions warrant removal, Congress must at least *consider* the full set of facts underlying those actions.

The first principle of due process is that the arbiter of a dispute must evaluate all facts relevant to the accused's defense. The Democrats are, instead, systematically erasing them from the analysis.

The Republicans, meanwhile, are clinging to the delusion that Trump "did nothing wrong." But their frantic repetition of those words do not make them true. Notwithstanding the complications from the Bidens' connections to Burisma, Trump's actions were scandalous. The President of the United States should not—under any circumstances—withhold vitally important military aid from a vulnerable ally while pressing for targeted investigations into his chief political rival.

Sorry Republicans: This, too, is not nothing.

While it's an open question, before the Senate trial, whether Trump's acts were grave enough to warrant removal from office, they were undeniably reckless and improper. The Republicans, nonetheless, stridently march forward in their allegiance to the party line, insisting Trump's acts were par for the presidential course.

If Trump was genuinely concerned about the Bidens' actions regarding Ukraine he should have, at most, requested a broad and even-handed investigation into Ukrainian corruption generally, conducted above board and through legitimate government channels. Given that there was no evidence the Bidens committed any wrongdoing—but, rather, simply had a conflict of interest—the prudent course was to leave the whole thing alone.

The Republicans, however, simply brush this aside and—in a stunning act of collective self-deception—insist, again and again, that Trump did nothing wrong.

Both the Democrats and the Republicans need to come to grips with reality. The relevant facts on impeachment are complicated, messy, and as yet inconclusive. Right now only a few stray fragments of the relevant underlying facts are known publicly. And the constitutional standard for what qualifies as a high crime or misdemeanor in this context is murky.

Whether to remove the President of the United States from office is the biggest constitutional question of this generation. The stakes are too high for Congress to be in a state of denial.

JANUARY 15, 2020
THE REPUBLICANS' FOUR "KEY" FACTS
ON IMPEACHMENT

THE Republicans' central impeachment theme so far is this: The facts are on President Trump's side. Specifically, they have said (again and again) that, as Rep. Jim Jordan of Ohio put it, "four key facts will not change, have not changed, will never change."

Jordan somehow manages to keep a straight face while uttering this assertion.

For even if the four "key" facts are accepted as true, they are immaterial to the Democrats' charge that Trump abused his power. Put another way, the Republican's central theme on impeachment falls flat on its face. Let's take each one (using Jordan's formulation) in turn.

"Key Fact" Number One: "We have the transcript, there was no quid pro quo in the transcript."

Why would this matter? The "transcript" covers the July 25, 2019 phone call between Trump and Ukrainian President Volodymyr Zelensky. The Democrats' allegations are not that President Trump abused his power only on this specific phone call. If, for example, Trump pressured Ukraine to investigate the Bidens in exchange for receiving aid *after* he hung up with Zelensky (hours, days, or even weeks after), the Democrats' case would remain blissfully intact. The question is whether Trump abused his power over several months, not simply on the July 25 call.

"Key Fact" Number Two: "The two guys on the call,

President Trump and President Zelensky, both said 'no pressure, no pushing, no quid pro quo.'"

Hmmm. The fact that Trump denies pressuring Ukraine is neither surprising nor important. If simply denying an accusation were a sufficient defense, Anglo-American legal history would be devoid of convictions.

As for President Zelensky, well, just like in July, he still needs Trump's help. His country is, after all, at war with a much-larger Russia and thus desperately reliant on American money and other support. Zelensky is—to put it mildly— not a disinterested third-party witness: He has powerful incentives to please Trump, to nod his head, and to say "no pressure, no pushing, no quid pro quo." Taking any other approach risks disaster for his country.

"Key Fact" Number Three: "The Ukrainians, third, didn't know that the aid was held up at the time of the phone call."

This key fact runs headlong into the same problem as Key Fact Number One: The Democrats don't claim that Trump's abuse of power occurred only on a single phone call. If the Ukrainians found out that Trump held up the aid after the phone call (again: hours, days, or even weeks after), the Democrats' claims would be just as strong. As long as Ukraine found out before Trump released the aid in September—which this key fact seems to admit—what Ukraine knew on July 25 is insignificant.

"Key Fact" Number Four: "The Ukrainians never started, never promised to start, and never announced an investigation in the time that the aid was paused."

This appears to be true. But, again, why does this matter?

According to the Democrats, Trump got caught before Ukraine announced an investigation. That's their charge. The absence of Ukrainian action does not negate the Democrats' central contention—that Trump did act, and abused his power, by withholding aid and simultaneously pressuring Ukraine to announce an investigation.

The Republicans' four key facts, even if accepted as true, thus don't negate a single element of the Democrats' charges.

The best argument Republicans have is not rooted in the facts about Trump's behavior, which are grim to any honest observer. The best argument Republicans have is rooted in the law—namely, that while Trump did act highly improperly (just admit it, Republicans) his acts did not, quite, meet the high constitutional threshold for being a high crime or other misdemeanor.

While this argument might not roll off the tongue—or be easy to articulate in an angry tweet—it is far better than continuing to regurgitate four irrelevancies. For even if these four facts "will not change, have not changed, will never change," they are, still, a woefully deficient defense to the Democrats' allegations.

MARCH 3, 2020
THE ZERO-SUM IMPEACHMENT

S ENATE Republicans' refusal to hear from any witnesses was a final blow to an impeachment process riddled with fundamental deficiencies. Indeed, Democrats and Republicans in Congress treated President Trump's impeachment like any other zero-sum partisan contest even though both sides—and the nation as a whole—had an essential shared interest in the impartial pursuit of the truth.

The American people deserved better.

Two stunning statements from Congressional leaders illustrate how deeply flawed the process was. The first came from Sen. Majority Leader Mitch McConnell (a former judge), who explained before the trial even started that Republican senators would be in "total coordination with the White House counsel's office and the people who are representing the president in the well of the Senate." This of course turns the most elemental principle of fair trials—that jurors should not communicate, let alone coordinate, with a party—completely on its head.

Then came the second whopper. In a plea to Republican senators to allow U.S. Ambassador to Ukraine William Taylor's notes at trial, Rep. Adam Schiff righteously exclaimed that in "any courtroom in America holding a fair trial, you would want to see contemporaneous notes."

Schiff (a seasoned trial lawyer), as lead prosecutor in the House, denied the accused the right to counsel, the right to call witnesses central to relevant underlying events, and the right to confront his accusers. These rights are bedrock principles of fairness and due process and no judge in America holding a fair trial would deny them.

While both sides rationalized this partisan hardball by—surprise, surprise—saying it was the other side that was really the problem, this is not how Congress should have determined whether to take the largest constitutional step in our nation's history and, for the first time, remove a sitting president.

When historians look back on this impeachment they will uniformly condemn Trump's use of congressionally authorized funds to pressure Ukraine to investigate the Bidens. But those same historians will reserve sharp criticism for our elected officials in Congress, who turned solemn constitutional proceedings into hyper-partisan and results-oriented political sport.

The principles of fair proceedings that Congress systematically violated are not arbitrary constructs invented by the courts that can be discarded in impeachment proceedings simply because the judiciary is confined to a subsidiary role. They are fundamental bulwarks against unfairness and injustice that are deeply rooted in Anglo-American history, elementary logic, and a keen understanding of human nature.

Several examples establish the point. First, the right to counsel allows lay defendants who do not understand legal nuances to navigate complicated proceedings under the protections of attorney-client privilege. Second, the broad right to call witnesses who are squarely relevant to central underlying events secures both sides the opportunity to put on a robust case. And, finally, the bright-line rule that jurors may not communicate with a party outside of court is an essential prerequisite to the jury performing the most sacred function of all: rendering an impartial verdict.

These rules (and others like them) are indispensable restraints on the passions inherent in heated adversarial proceedings. Yet with the executive branch on trial and the judiciary on the sideline, an unrestrained Congress cast them aside.

Today, each party blames the other for the numerous affronts to impartial justice. History, on the other hand, will be kind to neither side.

2/ THE BULWARK

"Presidents come and go, but the Supreme Court goes on forever."

—William Howard Taft, President of the United States (1909–1913) and Chief Justice of the Supreme Court (1921–1930)

AMERICAN democracy is backsliding in the Trump era. But some institutions have stayed sober and administered effective governance. The judiciary, for example, has largely kept America's essential principles front and center amid the political frenzy.

The Supreme Court has remained a rational body, even while producing occasional opinions that inflame one side of the political aisle or the other. (There's no way around that.) During Trump's presidency the Court saw 5-4 and (after Ruth Bader Ginsburg's death) 6-3 conservative majorities. Yet it ruled against Trump repeatedly, including in major cases involving the U.S. Census, Deferred Action for Childhood Arrivals (DACA), and LGBTQ rights. The Court, moreover, held that a New York prosecutor could have access to Trump's private business records while he was the sitting president. And after Trump's presidency the Court ordered the National Archives to turn over Trump's classified presidential records to the Congressional committee investigating the January 6, 2021 riot at the United States Capitol. Most importantly, the Court rejected Trump's petitions to take up his baseless claims surrounding the 2020 presidential election.

The lower federal courts have likewise done an exemplary job in the Trump era. While judges vary ideologically, as expected in a two-party political system, the judiciary is, still, filled with bright and committed people. This is a testament not only to the caliber of lawyers and judges in America, but to the Senate confirmation process, which is a pivotal safeguard against unqualified people serving in important positions. As president, Trump was free to say whatever he wanted in a speech and to take counsel from the advisors of his choice. But he could not get judges or other officials confirmed by the Senate without the consent of numerous moderate Republican senators. Case in point: Among the many lower-court judges who flatly rejected Trump's post-election litigation campaign were several nominated by Trump himself.

Indeed, the American framers' decision to insulate the Judiciary from the political process, through lifetime appointments, has been, over two hundred years later, an essential bulwark against the ever-increasing partisanship in American politics. It is of course true that there is some amount of dysfunction in the judiciary. While the Senate has largely prevented unqualified people from serving as judges, the Republicans' refusal to hold hearings for Barack Obama's Supreme Court nominee Merrick Garland was an unfortunate deviation from historical practice. And—while far less than in the political branches—some partisanship does creep into the daily workings of federal courts. On the whole, however, federal judges have sustained a high level of functioning throughout the Trump years.

"The Judiciary," Alexander Hamilton wrote in *Federalist No. 78*, "has no influence over either the sword or the purse; no direction either of the strength or of the wealth of the society, and can take no active resolution whatever. It may truly be said to have neither FORCE nor WILL, but merely judgment." The judiciary continues to exercise that judgment well.

MAY 10, 2020
TRUMP VERSUS CONGRESS AND THE STATES:
ENTER THE SUPREME COURT

AFTER a long, arduous—and regrettable—impeachment process it's the Supreme Court's turn to get involved in the long-running battle between President Trump and Democrats in Congress. The Court will soon hear oral argument in three cases involving the constitutional limits of investigations into Trump.

Commenting on the Court in 1953, Justice Robert Jackson famously wrote, "We are not final because we are infallible, but we are infallible only because we are final." Justice Jackson recognized that the Court gets the last word on constitutional questions only because it sits atop the federal court system, not because the nine justices themselves have a monopoly on wisdom.

This is still true today. When it comes to our most important constitutional questions, the nine justices of the Court—for better or worse—decide the answer. Everyone else talks. And after a yearslong onslaught of competing opinions (mostly raw, partisan-driven assertions) about the proper balance between executive, legislative and state power during the Trump presidency, the Court is finally weighing in.

It's about time.

Given the Trump-induced mania in the elected branches of the federal government it is extraordinarily important that the judiciary—the only branch of government left—maintain sobriety and fidelity to the Constitution. The Supreme Court needs to get this right.

In two of the cases, Democrats in Congress seek President Trump's private business records for their ongoing investigations. In the third, the Manhattan District Attorney wants Trump's tax returns for his active criminal proceedings.

In resisting these efforts, Trump argues that the Court must protect him from harassment by an adversarial Congress and a hostile state prosecutor. Congress and the Manhattan District Attorney argue that, to the contrary, no president is above the law and they have legitimate legal bases for getting these records.

More important than these specific legal arguments, however, is the broader context. On the one hand, Trump has unprecedented entanglements between his private businesses and his public office—and a unique disregard for constitutional safeguards against presidential abuse of power. Trump, for instance, has referred to the Emoluments Clause in the Constitution—which prohibits a sitting president from receiving payments from foreign governments—as "the phony Emoluments Clause." Expressing a common narrative from the left, Rep. Jerrold Nadler (D-N.Y.) has called Trump "a dictator" who "must be removed from office."

On the other, Trump has already been investigated to an unprecedented degree. He endured both the Mueller investigation (which after two years did not find evidence he colluded with Russia to hack into the Democratic National Committee's email servers) and impeachment proceedings (after which he was acquitted). And numerous officials from his campaign and administration have been convicted of crimes. Expressing a common narrative from the right, Attorney General William Barr said that Democrats "essentially see themselves as engaged in a war to cripple, by any means necessary, a duly elected government."

These cases raise questions rooted in unprecedented times. But the ruling will apply for generations. If Joe Biden wins the presidency, the ruling will govern how Republicans can investigate his and his family's business dealings. It will apply in the future when a dishonest president squares off against a good-intentioned Congress. And it will apply—just the same—vice versa. Donald Trump won't be president forever. And permanently weakening the presidency in response to Trump's anomalous, yet temporary, incumbency would be a fundamental error. In America's constitutional system the things we do now are the rules we have to live by later.

Where, then, is the constitutional line drawn? Can the courts force a sitting president to hand over this sensitive private information to his adversaries? The Supreme Court is now—finally—involved. We will have the answer soon enough.

JUNE 26, 2020
GORSUCH STYMIES TRUMP

THE Supreme Court's recent opinion interpreting the Civil Rights Act is a comforting reminder of President Trump's consistent inability to accomplish his goals. The opinion was authored by Trump's first pick for the Supreme Court, Justice Neil Gorsuch. Flatly rejecting the Trump administration's arguments, Gorsuch held that the Civil Rights Act prevents employers from discriminating against gay and transgender employees.

Finally. Since 1964, Title VII of the Civil Rights Act has prohibited employers from discriminating against "any individual … because of such individual's … sex." Yet federal courts and numerous states have allowed employers to openly discriminate against gay and transgender employees.

No more. Justice Gorsuch said it plain: "An employer who fires an individual for being homosexual or transgender fires that person for traits or actions it would not have questioned in members of a different sex. Sex plays a necessary and undisguisable role in the decision, exactly what Title VII forbids."

In yet another dissenting opinion criticizing the Court for extending gay rights, Justice Samuel Alito (a vociferous critic of the Court's 2015 opinion recognizing gay marriage) asserted that neither "sexual orientation" nor "gender identity" appear in the Civil Rights Act, and therefore gay and transgender employees are afforded none of its protections. "Usurping the constitutional authority of the other branches," Alito lamented, the Court has legislated "under the guise of statutory interpretation. A more brazen abuse of our authority to interpret statutes is hard to recall."

Alito misses the point. Far from brazen, Gorsuch's interpretation is compelled by the Civil Rights Act's prohibition of discrimination based on a person's "sex."

Take a simple example. Under Alito's interpretation of the Civil Rights Act, if a man marries a woman that man is protected in the workplace. If a female marries the same woman, however, that female is not protected in the workplace. Only one thing changed: the *sex* of the person marrying the woman. Drawing a legal distinction between the two scenarios is thus solely predicated on a person's "sex," expressly contravening the Civil Rights Act's prohibition.

Echoing the Trump administration's arguments, Justice Alito asserts that this logic can be cast aside simply because the Civil Rights Act's drafters did not have gay and transgender people in mind in 1964.

But so what? The plain and ordinary meaning of the word "sex" controls, irrespective of present-day assumptions regarding legislative intent. As Gorsuch explained: "Those who adopted the Civil Rights Act might not have anticipated their work would lead to this particular result … But the limits of the drafters' imagination supply no reason to ignore the law's demands. When the express terms of a statute give us one answer and extratextual considerations suggest another, it's no contest. Only the written word is the law, and all persons are entitled to its benefit."

Trump's resounding defeat in this case won't stop his broader crusade against LGBT+ and minorities' rights. Indeed, shortly before the Court's opinion the Trump administration finalized a rule that—if it withstands judicial scrutiny—would authorize discriminating against LGBTQ people regarding health care and health insurance.

Fortunately, Trump's ability to achieve his goals is consistently undercut by his overreaching objectives and clumsy execution. Whether Trump is thwarted by a Democrat-led House of Representatives, investigated by his own executive branch, or ignored by state and local governments, the instrumentalities of government are consistently blunting his ambitions. With Gorsuch's latest opinion, Trump's own appointee to the Supreme Court has taken his turn.

JULY 8, 2020
UNDERSTANDING JOHN ROBERTS

JOHN Roberts is Donald Trump's opposite. Unlike the President, the Chief Justice is cautious, reflective and deeply respectful of the nuance and history underpinning America's constitutional system. In four recent major cases, where Roberts sided with the Court's more liberal justices, he displayed a virtue nowhere to be found in President Trump's DNA: moderation.

The surprising string of cases started when Roberts joined a majority of justices in holding that the Civil Rights Act's workforce protections protect gay and transgender employees. Supporting this dramatic increase in gay and transgender rights came as a surprise from Roberts, a political conservative and lifelong Catholic. But Robert's vote is consistent with a strong trend among the American people towards recognizing LGBTQ rights.

Next, Robert's joined the liberal justices in a 5-4 decision holding that DACA—the wildly popular Obama-era program protecting young Americans from deportation— must continue. There is a growing consensus in the U.S. that DACA recipients should be protected, even if the battle over immigration in other areas remains fierce. Roberts' vote prevented a raw, partisan majority of justices from terminating this popular program.

Roberts then joined the Court's liberals in striking down Louisiana's law requiring abortion doctors to have admitting privileges in local hospitals. Just four years ago, in a nearly identical case, the Court held the same thing. Roberts' vote prevented a simple change in personnel (Justice Kavanaugh replacing Justice Kennedy) from flipping the Court to the opposite conclusion. Continuity in the Court's jurisprudence—a touchstone of judicial moderation—was Roberts' guiding principle.

Finally, in the last case of the term, Roberts rejected Trump's argument that he, as president, is immune from basic legal processes. Roberts' opinion authorized the Manhattan District Attorney to continue seeking Trump's tax returns. In doing so, Roberts emphatically reaffirmed the principle that no person—even the president—is above the law.

Roberts explained his overarching judicial philosophy during his 2005 Senate confirmation. "Judges have to have the humility to recognize that they operate within a system of precedent shaped by other judges equally striving to live up to the judicial oath, and judges have to have modesty to be open in the decisional process to the considered views of their colleagues on the bench."

Roberts' willingness to forgo short-term political victories in the name of broader, long-term considerations starkly contrasts with President Trump. Roberts' November 2018 response to Trump slandering a federal judge as an "Obama judge" highlights the differences between the two men: "We do not have Obama judges or Trump judges, Bush judges or Clinton judges. What we have is an extraordinary group of dedicated judges doing their level best to do equal right to those appearing before them."

Donald Trump has spent his presidency sowing divisiveness and waging a zero-sum battle for narrow, party-line victories. He has cast aside long-term principles that hold America's constitutional system of government together. And he has rattled the American people with one knee-jerk partisan maneuver after another. With this string of cases, John Roberts reminds us that sanity and rationality still exist in government. He is doing what he can to calm the storm.

3/ THE PEOPLE AND THE PRESS

"A lie can travel around the world and back again while the truth is lacing up its boots."

—*Attributed to Mark Twain*

DONALD Trump and politicians from both political parties have stress tested American democracy in recent years. But elected officials are not the only culprits. Many in the press, and much of the populace, have also consistently abandoned American democracy's core principles.

The cause is threefold. First, Americans are often uninformed about and indifferent to the workings of their government. America's unprecedented peace and prosperity has created generations of people who simply have other concerns. Some Americans are busy focusing on socially redeeming activities in, for example, business, academia, or philanthropy. Others face challenges in life that consume their bandwidth and prevent them from focusing on civic matters. Still others are simply uninterested and focus on other things like sports and entertainment.

This indifference has consequences. As Plato said long ago: "One of the penalties for refusing to participate in politics is that you end up being governed by your inferiors."

Second, Americans, like all people, are plagued by biased thinking. In a country drowning in low-quality information, disoriented by the computerized echo chambers of social media, and afflicted by overheated tribal passions, bias runs rampant. A huge percentage of Americans embrace wholesale whatever facts are consistent with their tribal preferences—whatever the source—while flatly rejecting anything inconsistent with their worldview. How assertions of fact make people *feel* as opposed to whether they are *true* typically drives people's beliefs.

Finally, an often-partisan press—fixated on clicks and motivated by profits—fans the flames. Put simply, the modern media juices the flywheel of American irrationality. It focuses disproportionately on flashy, negative events, ignoring slow-moving but important developments. And it prefers scandal over substance. The media itself is, of course, simply one subset of the American people (that subset with a public microphone) and it, too, is afflicted by all the same dysfunctions as the populace itself.

As the columns in this chapter illustrate, government officials are not the only actors stress testing American democracy.

JULY 18, 2020
WHAT AMERICA'S GOOGLE SEARCHES SAY ABOUT
ITS PRIORITIES

WITH over 90 percent market share in internet search, Google is a dominant way for Americans to seek and receive information about the world. Google Trends keeps track of all the searches and provides tools for analyzing the data.

The search statistics show that Americans have a stunning indifference to fundamentally important subjects and, at the same time, a gross infatuation with triviality. The idea that Americans' focus may often be misguided is nothing new. But with Google Trends, we now have massive troves of hard data substantiating the thesis.

Several examples illustrate the point.

Take, first, a comparison between Americans' interest in the multi-trillion-dollar federal budget and in reality television. The United States budget reflects America's core national values and objectively measures its global impact. Given its size and scope, the budget materially alters billions of lives both at home and abroad.

Google Trends shows, however, that Americans care more—far more—about the inconsequential happenings of strangers than they do about how our trillions are deployed. There is, for example, tremendously more interest in the "Real Housewives of Beverly Hills" than in the Office of Management and Budget, the executive agency that oversees budgetary spending—peaking at over 10 times the interest when the housewife drama gets particularly juicy.

And how about the House Ways and Means Committee—which writes the u.s. tax code—compared to "Vanderpump Rules"? It's worse—peaking at roughly 100 times more interest in Vanderpump.

Even Speaker of the House Nancy Pelosi gets unceremoniously brushed aside when "The Bachelorette" is in season—typically peaking at roughly 25–50 times more interest in "The Bachelorette."

Another example of the staggering disconnect between what Americans are interested in and what matters is a comparison between the Kardashian family (Kim, Kanye, Kylie, and the gang) and Africa (yes, the entire continent). Despite making great progress in recent decades, Africa continues to have widespread and profound challenges. Much of the continent—still traumatized by a long history of foreign interference and endless war—is perennially ravaged by preventable hunger, economic distress, and child mortality.

Yet Americans care more—far more—about the Kardashians than all of the countries in Africa.

Combined.

Take a comparison in Google searches between Kim Kardashian and The Democratic Republic of Congo, a country of 80-plus million people with a brutal history of colonialism and industrial exploitation. The results are startling—peaking at roughly 100 times more interest in Kim.

Kim's sister Kylie Jenner versus Mozambique? Same thing—peaking at well over 100 times more interest in Kylie.

And Kim's husband Kanye West and Ghana? You guessed it—peaking at about 50 times more interest in Kanye.

Additional examples abound. There's Meghan Markle (the wife of England's Prince Harry) versus Theresa May (the country's recent prime minister). Jussie Smollett (at the peak of the previously little-known actor's fake-battery scandal) versus China (yes, China). Deflategate (Tom Brady's deflated-football controversy) versus the Federal Reserve (yes, the Fed).

And so on.

Google Trends is, indeed, a data-driven window into the conscience of America. The results speak for themselves.

This misfocus is not just disappointing—It has consequences. Apathy and inattention are the engine of corruption and abuse. America's budget deficit is set to reach $1 trillion next year at the same time massive addressable problems such as child homelessness, crumbling infrastructure, and under-performing public schools compound negatively at accelerating speeds.

And despite being the richest country on earth, America has the least generous foreign-aid contribution of any developed nation. Just a fraction of the extreme wealth of the top 0.1% of Americans (capital which compounds positively at accelerating speeds) could save tens of millions of lives in Africa.

Put simply, when Americans focus on the wrong things, the wrong things happen. When Americans do not pay attention to how tax dollars are spent, catastrophic waste and abuse occurs. When Americans ignore entire continents screaming for help, widespread death results.

And, indeed, when Americans care more about reality television than the federal government, a reality television star gets elected president.

JULY 22, 2020
COGNITIVE DISSONANCE IN AMERICAN POLITICS

COGNITIVE dissonance occurs when new information that conflicts with someone's deeply held beliefs causes that person to feel mental discomfort. It is prevalent in people who believe sweeping false narratives based upon incomplete information.

In these partisan times where both sides of the political aisle regularly embrace storylines that are consistent with preconceived notions—but inconsistent with the facts—cognitive dissonance is a widespread affliction. The events from several months ago, on February 14, 2020, relating to Attorney General William Barr, illustrate the point.

On this noteworthy day the following happened: (1) Barr criticized President Trump on ABC News for tweeting about active Department of Justice criminal cases; (2) Barr appointed an outside prosecutor to review the FBI's investigation into and DOJ's prosecution of Trump's former National Security Advisor Michael Flynn; and (3) the DOJ announced that it would not pursue charges against former FBI Acting Director Andrew McCabe.

That's a lot to take in at once.

To diehard Trump supporters who—before February 14th—viewed Barr as a loyal Trump deputy on a campaign to right the many wrongs inflicted upon Trump by the "Deep State," these three things could not be squared. Why would the dependable Barr criticize his leader, especially in public? And why would McCabe, a deep-state bureaucrat who (along with his boss James Comey) covertly kick-started the Russian Witch Hunt, get a pass from Barr's DOJ?

To diehard Trump opponents who—before February 14th—viewed Barr as Trump's political henchman, brazenly weaponizing the DOJ to pursue Trump's perceived enemies and political opponents, these three things likewise could not be harmonized. Why would the subservient Barr openly criticize a president he has steadfastly protected? And why would Barr's DOJ disobey Trump's command to prosecute McCabe?

The cognitive dissonance—the incompatibility of these facts with the existing narratives—was acute.

How, indeed, could all of these things happen at once? The answer is simple: The truth about Trump's relationship with Barr and the DOJ is multifaceted, complicated, and largely not public. The standard narratives about Trump and Barr are too simple. As Nobel Laureate psychologist Daniel Kahneman explained, "If people can construct a simple and coherent story, they will feel confident regardless of how well grounded it is in reality." All outsiders can do with Trump and Barr, as a practical matter, is draw inferences based upon limited and imperfect knowledge.

This, of course, is very unsatisfying to concerned partisans who crave clear, simple narratives that confirm their worldview. So what do they do? They preserve their narratives by filling in the ambiguous factual void with their own preconceived notions. Preconceived notions rooted in strong ideological preference, however, inevitably contain false judgments. As Arthur Schopenhauer famously said, "Every man takes the limits of his own field of vision for the limits of the world." His point—vividly illustrated on February 14th—was that the world is much larger than what people perceive, and that reality is often far different from what people believe.

To the impartial, cognitive dissonance is a warning signal that triggers reflection and mental adjustment. To the partisan, by contrast, cognitive dissonance is a nuisance remedied by diminishing or distorting the new and inconsistent facts. The latter was on display on February 14th, when many people focused disproportionately on the Flynn news, which was harmonious with most existing narratives, or quickly embraced fanciful theories that Trump secretly authorized Barr's public criticism.

The optimal way to respond to new information is to flexibly adjust one's views to the changing body of established evidence. This approach is not common in an era of overconfident zealotry. And it certainly doesn't eliminate human misjudgment. But it does guard against the oversimplifications that lead to cognitive dissonance and, therefore, make days like February 14th a little less jarring.

JULY 31, 2020
ANECDOTES, ABERRATIONS AND AVERAGES

CONTEXT matters. Take this simple statement: Nearly ten percent of the world's people live in extreme poverty.

This is true. And standing alone, without context, this statement would lead many to think the world has a huge poverty problem. They'd be right. But they'd also be missing a big part of the story: Just twenty-five years ago nearly 30 percent of people lived in extreme poverty.

So the world's extreme poverty problem is actually getting much better.

The prospects for the future would be very different if instead of steadily improving extreme poverty was stagnating at nearly ten percent. Or, worse, if extreme poverty was steadily increasing. But there's no way of knowing which of these distinct scenarios is true from the statement alone.

You need context.

Terrorism is another good example of how context matters. The events of September 11, 2001 highlighted the great dangers of terrorism. But how does terrorism compare to other threats? While terrorists have killed about 3,000 Americans since 2000, over 20,000 Americans die by homicide or murder annually. And more than 38,000 die from traffic accidents each year.

Is terrorism, in context, as threatening as some think? Did it make sense for the federal government to create the mammoth Department of Homeland Security after 9-11 while underfunding pandemic preparedness the last two decades?

Hardly.

There are subtler examples, too. President Trump loves to brag about the stock market setting "records." "The Dow Jones reached a new record on my watch" is a common boast from Trump. But looking at the stock market in context shows—surprise, surprise—Trump's statements are highly misleading. The stock market is a cumulative tally—it never resets to zero. It also always goes up over time because, on average, publicly traded companies get bigger as they mature. A new market high is a very different record from, say, baseball's single-season homerun record, which requires extraordinary performance. In stark contrast, the stock market can break records even while increasing at below-average rates.

People embrace facts out of context all the time. (And not just Donald Trump.) They disregard trend lines. They ignore the net impact of something and focus on discrete effects. They gloss over comparables and instead focus on isolated samples. They confuse outliers and aberrations with the mean or the median. And many have trouble with scale, hardly distinguishing 100 million units of something from a billion units.

Anecdotal thinking is particularly widespread. People often tell stories that support their worldview without considering the big picture. Global warming deniers, like Trump, describe dramatic blizzards to show that the world is not warming. But to know whether there's global warming you need to know, well, whether the globe is warming—not how much snow there was in Green Bay last December 18. And the data clearly establishes that Earth, on the whole, is getting hotter. In many cases, like global warming, context is not just important—it is a necessary precondition to understanding something at all.

Harvard professor Steven Pinker wonders why humanity "appears to be losing its mind." How can the same species "that developed vaccines for Covid-19 in less than a year," Pinker asks, "produce so much fake news, medical quackery, and conspiracy theorizing?"

We do indeed have a rationality problem. And it's causing significant challenges to American democracy. One of the core reasons why is that people draw the wrong conclusions about what they see. Again and again. Taking the time to put things in context would help.

A lot.

AUGUST 2, 2020
FACTS VERSUS NARRATIVES

People have a tendency to interpret new facts as being consistent with their strongly held beliefs. This propensity, known as confirmation bias, is well known. What is not generally appreciated, however, is that confirmation bias is not just a mild affliction. It is a dominating factor in human thinking—especially with far-off matters distant from one's direct personal experience.

Nobel prize-winning cognitive psychologist Daniel Kahneman explained that "confirmation bias comes from when you have an interpretation, and you adopt it, and then, top down, you force everything to fit that interpretation." And Karl Popper noted that "if we are uncritical we shall always find what we want: we shall look for, and find, confirmations, and we shall look away from, and not see, whatever might be dangerous to our pet theories."

Confirmation bias has two basic components. First, we embrace and amplify facts that confirm our existing narratives. And second, we resist and diminish evidence that's inconsistent with our narratives.

Confirmation bias is endemic in politics. And it's getting worse. Today's unprecedented partisanship largely results from the toxic mixture of confirmation bias and an explosion of information. The Internet is an elaborate menu allowing people to pick and choose what they want to believe.

The examples of confirmation bias in politics are endless. Conservatives, for instance, often celebrate the "Trump economy," citing the stock market as a principal reason why President Trump runs the economy significantly better than President Obama. The fact that the stock market increased 150% under Obama (and has increased significantly less under Trump) is typically missing from the presentation.

Sure, Trump has been president less than half as long as Obama was. And grading economic performance requires looking beyond simply the stock market. But to ignore Obama's historically impressive stock market record—while touting Trump's performance—is confirmation bias on full display.

On the other side of the aisle, there is a constant liberal drumbeat that Trump is soft on Russia. But Trump has sanctioned Russia repeatedly; expelled Russian diplomats from the us; sold arms to Russian foe Ukraine; and aggressively opposed Russia's effort to build a lucrative oil pipeline into Europe. And Trump ordered the bombing of Russian ally Syria—where Russia's military maintains a significant presence—prompting Vladimir Putin to call the strikes an "act of aggression" that could "have a destructive effect on the entire system of international relations."

True, Trump's relationship with Russia is complicated and his behavior regarding Putin raises legitimate concerns. But to ignore the numerous hard lines Trump has drawn with Russia distorts and oversimplifies the story.

As Charlie Munger noted, Charles Darwin "always gave priority attention to evidence tending to disconfirm whatever cherished and hard-won theory he already had. In contrast, most people early achieve and later intensify a tendency to process new and disconfirming information so that any original conclusion remains intact."

Darwin's approach of resisting confirmation bias and seeking facts that *conflict* with our own narratives is optimal. Giving a fair shake to disconfirming evidence forces us to concede our pet theory is wrong when the facts demand it—which isn't easy for prideful humans. But doing so is, after all, far better than continuing to embrace a false narrative.

AUGUST 9, 2020
THE FRENEMY OF THE PEOPLE

PRESIDENT Trump's frequent claim that the media is "the enemy of the people" is dangerous and absurd. But that doesn't mean it is the people's best friend. The media is, instead, more like the frenemy of the people: Its impact on society is a mix of good and bad.

The media's positive impact on society is well understood (in part because journalists constantly talk about it). The media is, to be sure, a fundamental bulwark against concentrated power—in both the government and the private sector—that consistently exposes important facts. This is particularly important now given Trump's incessant attacks on America's core customs and institutions. The media also, at its best, produces high-quality analysis about significant subjects.

The media's negative impact on society is less understood (in part because journalists don't talk about it much). Its deficiencies, however, are fundamental.

First, the media is partisan. A strong majority of journalists are liberal; there's a robust conservative minority; and in between is a slim apolitical middle. This mix of ideologies interacts in a modern-media ecosystem that has devolved into a fragmented echo chamber of bias and prejudgment.

The near-unlimited menu of news content—on television, radio, the Internet, and print—allows people to gravitate towards what they want. It also insulates them from what they don't want. The hyper-partisanship of modern times rages on because most people rarely confront the unfiltered views of those with whom they disagree.

Second, the media's incentive structure is misaligned. Journalists' goals are often at odds with accurate reporting. They are motivated to become famous; to win awards; to create buzzworthy headlines; to sell the news. Boring stories that objectively explain slow-moving or unexciting subject matter—no matter how important—do not generate excitement. And positive or congratulatory articles about people in power—no matter how impressive their accomplishments—are snoozers likely to be ignored.

Controversy sells. (Just look who got elected president.) Substance means little. (Just look who got elected president.) The bigger the controversy, the more eyeballs; the more eyeballs, the more clicks; the more clicks, the more advertising revenue. And so on. This flywheel has accelerated exponentially in the modern age of unlimited content, deep fragmentation, and decreasing media-company profit margins. The 24-hour news cycle is fueled not by thorough and objective analysis but instead by the snap-shot partisanship that people crave.

And this leads to disproportionate focus on negative, attention-grabbing stories. As *New York Times* journalist Nicholas Kristof wrote: "We journalists are a bit like vultures, feasting on war, scandal and disaster. Turn on the news, and you see Syrian refugees, Volkswagen corruption, dysfunctional government. Yet that reflects a selection bias in how we report the news: We cover planes that crash, not planes that take off."

Finally, the media produces oversimplified narratives.

By its very nature—short and abbreviated explanations of large and complicated subject matter—much of today's journalism is misleading and lacks context.

It is essential that the public is apprised of important facts regarding society. All too often, however, journalists weave these facts into incomplete or inaccurate storylines. Waiting for all the facts to emerge when your competition already tweeted its headline is simply not an option. It took Robert Mueller two years to opine on the Trump campaign's ties to Russia. The media did not have that luxury.

The frenetic competition to generate more clicks—to perpetually fill the 24-hour news cycle with stimulating content—forces media institutions to publish the best of what's known, even if it's only the tip of the iceberg. Put simply: You publish the story you have, not the story you might want.

Despite these problems, the media is not the enemy of the people. It is, instead, the frenemy of the people: It serves an indispensable function in American democracy while, at the same time, having its own set of deficiencies. Trump's criticism of the media goes way too far. But those who underplay its systemic problems have it wrong, too.

4/ CRIMINAL JUSTICE REFORM

"The true measure of our character is how we treat the poor, the disfavored, the accused, the incarcerated, and the condemned."

—*Bryan Stevenson*

Another key aspect of America's stress test is its dysfunctional criminal-justice system. Antithetical to the American ideals of rationality and equality, a huge number of Americans—disproportionately people from underprivileged backgrounds—are trapped in a senseless system of mass incarceration. Put simply, far too many Americans are in jail for far too long. And, while imprisoned, they are often subject to brutal and inhumane conditions.

America's criminal-justice system thus consistently violates the essential American principle of proportional punishment. The punishment is supposed to fit the crime. When, instead, the punishment is too long or too severe, gratuitous harm is inflicted on vulnerable people.

Moreover, because many people with criminal records are not allowed to vote, mass incarceration distorts the franchise, preventing truly free and fair elections. Indeed, political battles over the voting rights of people with criminal records consistently determine election outcomes.

The failures of America's criminal-justice system have led to much of the country's recent civil unrest and social division. And understandably so. Oppressed and disenfranchised communities are, predictably, often deep wells of anger and resentment. And the problem is not simply high-profile incidents captured on camera, like George Floyd's May 25, 2020 murder at the hands of a Minneapolis police officer. Many underserved communities have been slowly and quietly decimated over time—year after year, decade after decade—by the cumulative toll of America's legal system.

It's hardly surprising people are angry. As Frederick Douglass said, "Where justice is denied, where poverty is enforced, where ignorance prevails, and where any one class is made to feel that society is an organized conspiracy to oppress, rob and degrade them, neither persons nor property will be safe."

AUGUST 17, 2020
PRISON REFORM IN THE AGE OF COVID-19

PRESIDENT Trump's coronavirus press conferences include
lots of numbers. But one data set is being ignored: Over
60,000 prisoners in the United States have been infected
with Covid-19. And the number of infections is rising at
an alarming rate. This gratuitous suffering and death is a
tragedy.

The widespread release of vulnerable and nonviolent
prisoners must happen. Right now.

Yet the Covid-19 emergency only scratches the surface
of the deficiencies in the American prison system. It has
numerous fundamental problems.

First, the conditions in us prisons have long been terrible.
They are often overcrowded, under-resourced, and, lacking
in concerned public scrutiny, without proper oversight.

In 2019, for example, Trump's Department of Justice
issued a harrowing report detailing the conditions in
Alabama's prisons. "The violations are severe, systemic, and
exacerbated by serious deficiencies in staffing and supervi-
sion." There was, the DOJ continued, "a high level of violence that is too common, cruel, of an unusual nature, and
pervasive."

Nowhere in America's laws does criminal punishment
include violence, disease, and (other than with capital
offenses) even death. Yet for America's prisoners they are fre-
quently a gratuitous part of the equation. Covid-19 merely
compounds an already existing problem.

Second, the court system is fundamentally flawed. As a result, many innocent people go to prison—and guilty people are often there far too long. Wealthy defendants receive high-quality representation while poor ones get overworked public defenders. Prosecutors enjoy broad discretion and immunity for bad acts. And juries—the linchpin of the entire system—are prone to bias and questionable convictions.

Finally, the prison system broadly and disproportionately harms impoverished communities and reinforces socioeconomic disparities. America imprisons well over two million people and has more people behind bars per capita than any other nation. Unsurprisingly, inmates are disproportionately from poor communities. It's hard to fathom, but George Floyd, had he not been killed by the police during his arrest, quite possibly would be sitting in jail right now. Nothing compounds injustice and inequality like excessively locking up people from disadvantaged neighborhoods.

These systemic problems with our prisons—horrible conditions, flawed judicial proceedings, uneven socioeconomic impacts—interact with and compound each other. The whole is worse than the sum of the (already dismal) parts. And the net impact is staggering: Vast numbers of vulnerable citizens are sent to prison on questionable grounds where they are punished disproportionately and kept apart from their aching communities.

When it comes to the US prison system, the damage being done by Covid-19 is merely a symptom. The disease itself is much larger. We don't just need to release some nonviolent offenders. We need fundamental reform.

AUGUST 24, 2020
IMPRISONMENT DURING THE PANDEMIC IS CRUEL
AND UNUSUAL PUNISHMENT

THE Eighth Amendment to the Constitution of the
United States prohibits cruel and unusual punishment.
It states: "Excessive bail shall not be required, nor excessive fines imposed, nor cruel and unusual punishments
inflicted."

The Supreme Court has construed "cruel and unusual
punishments" to include certain forms of torture, such as
drawing and quartering. Yet the Court has allowed the death
penalty—which is still legal in dozens of states—to continue,
with some restrictions. In sum, the Eighth Amendment prohibits criminal punishments that are very harmful to prisoners and also rare or unprecedented.

Right now, over two million inmates sit locked inside US
prisons, where the novel coronavirus is rapidly spreading.
They are confined in close quarters and typically unable
to practice physical distancing. They are, moreover, at the
mercy of prison officials when it comes to receiving protective equipment and medical attention. A huge percentage
of these prisoners will be infected with the virus. A subset
of those infected will get severe symptoms. And a subset of
those with severe symptoms will die. Each and every inmate
will suffer the torment of not knowing where she or he will
ultimately fit into that equation.

Is confining people under these deadly and unprecedented
conditions cruel and unusual punishment? Put another way:

Is imprisonment during the coronavirus very harmful to prisoners and also unprecedented?

Yes, of course.

What, then, should the authorities do when a punishment becomes cruel and unusual not by an affirmative act of the state but instead by a global pandemic?

The wholesale release of all prisoners is obviously not a practical option. Among other concerns, the risk to public safety of such an approach—which would include setting free individuals convicted of violent offenses and even murder—is too great. And the political opposition to such a drastic move would be immense.

At the same time, taking only incremental steps is not viable either. Those in charge of federal and state prisons must recognize not just the grave health risks to prisoners and the moral imperative to protect them, but also the constitutional implications of their confinement. The Eighth Amendment prohibits this harrowing situation from continuing.

President Trump, Attorney General William Barr and other federal and state officials must accordingly do a full-court press to alleviate virus-induced pain and suffering in prisons. They must optimize the balance between public safety on the one hand and protecting the lives and constitutional rights of prisoners on the other.

Above all, President Trump—who has claimed to be a champion of criminal justice—must stop obsessing over how his response to the coronavirus is impacting the polls and instead focus on important problems like this one. Releasing non-violent offenders is a necessary and fundamental part of this process. Some prisons have begun doing so. But the scope and speed of the releases must immediately and dramatically increase.

The Supreme Court has explained that the Eighth Amendment "must draw its meaning from the evolving standards of decency that mark the progress of a maturing society." Only an immature and indecent society would casually leave vulnerable citizens—even those convicted of crimes—within the close quarters of a prison in the midst of a global pandemic.

The coronavirus is cruel. It is also unusual. And sitting in prison waiting to be infected is cruel and unusual punishment. America must aggressively release nonviolent prisoners on a broad scale across the country. Now.

SEPTEMBER 2, 2020
PRESIDENT TRUMP MUST DO MORE ON CRIMINAL JUSTICE REFORM

PRESIDENT Trump's criminal-justice reform efforts have been a positive for a president who has otherwise damaged America's legal system. The First Step Act, which Trump signed into law in 2018, takes several moderate steps to reform federal prisons, improve sentencing laws, and decrease the inmate population.

But what about the two million-plus Americans who remain in jail? What about the hundreds of thousands serving multi-year sentences for nonviolent offenses? And what about former inmates still handicapped by the myriad harmful effects of serving time?

These millions of Americans—and their millions of loved ones—are anxiously awaiting Trump's next move. To fulfill his repeated promise to fundamentally reform the criminal justice system, Trump must do a lot more than sign the First Step Act into law.

He must first address the impact of the coronavirus on prisons. A prison these days is even more dangerous than normal: One in five prisoners has contracted the virus. Nearly 2,000 have died. Nonviolent offenders should be released broadly and all prisoners should receive the vaccine on the same timeline as everyone else. Taking these steps would establish the basic premise on which meaningful criminal justice reform rests: that people who are in jail are just as important as people who are free.

Trump should then broaden his focus. Over two million people are imprisoned in America—the highest incarceration rate in the world. America spends roughly $182 billion annually to lock up a tragic percentage of its adult population.

It is of course true that some people belong in prison, particularly chronically recidivist or violent offenders. But an enormous number of Americans are in prison who shouldn't be. Trump should take three initial steps to address this problem.

First, Trump must lead a legislative effort to eliminate mandatory minimum sentences. Mandatory minimums require judges to sentence defendants convicted of certain crimes to minimum—and usually excessive—sentences. This system eliminates the essential discretion traditionally vested in judges to sentence people in careful proportion to their specific offenses.

Second, Trump and Congress must direct significant resources to enhance the representation of underprivileged defendants. America's overburdened public defenders cannot adequately navigate the complicated thicket of American justice. As civil rights attorney Bryan Stevenson put it: "Our criminal justice system treats you better if you are rich and guilty than if you are poor and innocent."

Third, Trump's Department of Justice must improve conditions in state-run jails. America does not just send too many people to jail. Once imprisoned, inmates are often subject to unthinkable abuse and neglect. The DOJ must aggressively supervise and investigate state-run jails and, when necessary, enforce meaningful changes.

Taking these steps would put a dent in America's mass

incarceration problem. But it would only be a start. Fundamentally improving the system is an uphill battle. People in jail can't vote, making them an easily dismissed political constituency. And a huge percentage of Americans harbor a reflexive law-and-order ideology resistant to reform.

Human beings in jail are just as important as those who are free. And battling the tens of millions of Americans who reject that view takes courage and hard work. The First Step Act was an incremental move in the right direction.

It's now time to start the heavy lifting.

5/ THE GATHERING STORM

"Is there no virtue among us? If there be not, we are in a wretched situation."

—*James Madison*

THE American people were on high alert in the months leading up to the November 2020 presidential election. It was a long summer. Fresh off being impeached, Donald Trump was sowing the seeds of the "Big Lie," blasting election-fraud falsehoods from his presidential megaphone. In July 2020, for example, he tweeted: "With Universal Mail-In Voting (not Absentee Voting, which is good), 2020 will be the most INACCURATE & FRAUDULENT Election in history."

His supporters were being whipped into a frenzy.

His opponents were tired, anxious, and angry.

An August, 2020 Gallup poll showed that only 13% of Americans were satisfied with the way things were going in the United States, the lowest percentage since the financial crash of 2009. One result of this national condition was a steady stream of overreactions. Many were worried that American democracy, after more than 200 years, was on the brink of extinction. There was even widespread concern that a civil war would break out. And there was an overarching fear that Trump—persistently labeled a dictator—would not leave the White House if he lost the election.

These opinions weren't commensurate with the facts. As the columns that follow illustrate, among the irrationalities of the Trump age is a fraying sense of proportion, even among well-educated Americans.

SEPTEMBER 5, 2020
IS AMERICAN DEMOCRACY IN JEOPARDY?

Is American democracy—the most successful political experiment in history—hanging on by a thread? Many commentators think so.

Thomas Friedman, a three-time Pulitzer Prize winner, warned that "the 2020 election may be the end of our democracy" and we may have "another Civil War." Columnist Robin Abcarian asserted that only one thing has saved the United States (and the world) from a Trump dictatorship: the ACLU. And Donald Trump is regularly called an "existential threat" to our democratic institutions.

Are they right? Is American democracy really teetering on the brink of extinction?

No. The punditry—and much of the country—has gone too far.

Things are, to be sure, really bad. An ignorant, bloviating reality-television star is president. A global pandemic is raging. California is burning. And our democratic salvation—the ballot box—is at the center of a firestorm.

Americans have, moreover, endured one limit-busting catastrophe after another—fraying our nerves and rattling our collective psychology. Americans did not think Candidate Trump could ever become Nominee Trump; we did not think Nominee Trump could ever become President Trump; we did not think an emerging China could ever become a rival China; and we did not think a virus could ever become a pandemic.

If these limits can be shattered then American democracy can be shattered, too, right?

No. There are hard limits to America's national downside. American democracy is enduring a stress test with Trump. But it isn't going anywhere.

Consider some facts.

Two years after Trump was elected the Democrats won a sweeping victory and took control of the House of Representatives. They have, ever since, stymied Trump's legislative agenda, relegating him largely to symbolic, impotent executive orders. They have investigated his administration at length. They have impeached him. And in the Senate, the filibuster endures—further blunting Trump's legislative ambitions.

The courts, moreover, have ruled against Trump consistently. A lower-level court halted Trump's Muslim Travel Ban (after his attorney general refused to enforce it). The Supreme Court rejected his attempt to reverse DACA and his anti-LGBT+ Civil Rights Act arguments. And the Court later held that a local prosecutor can seek Trump's personal financial records—something fundamentally inconsistent with the notion of dictatorship. Importantly, Trump has not violated a single court decision or questioned the legitimacy of the judicial branch as the last word on constitutional questions.

Even Trump's own executive branch has investigated him for years, sending numerous members of his team to jail. Just last week the Department of Justice indicted his former campaign manager and senior advisor Steve Bannon.

State and local governments have likewise protected and

defended our democratic institutions, rejecting overreaching Trump policies and mounting strong and consistent opposition in the courts and the public square.

The media, for its part, has been on overdrive since 2016, investigating Trump and his administration with unprecedented strength and vigor. The very fact that so many commentators openly call Trump a dictator with impunity proves that he is not one.

The military has not started a new war under Trump, let alone engaged in dictatorial conquest. (Trump's futile attempt to enlarge the country by purchasing Iceland was met with laughter throughout his administration.) And the idea that the military might splinter into two and fight a civil war is—with all due respect to Mr. Friedman—absurd. The military remains a respected and cohesive institution firmly under civilian control irrespective of which party holds the White House.

Trump is not an existential threat to America's democratic institutions. He is a test for them. And—under immense pressure—they are showing their strength.

It is true that our nation is experiencing great hardship. As we have before. One of our founding principles was slavery. It took a century—and a Civil War—to expunge it. Then came Jim Crow. Women's suffrage arrived just a century ago. We fought in two world wars, another in Korea, and another in Vietnam. We faced a pandemic in 1918. A Great Depression a decade later. And just ten years ago we confronted the near-collapse of our financial system.

America improves with time—but the slog is long and the trajectory nonlinear.

Things are bad now. And they very well may get worse. Even the best possible version of November will be a white-knuckled roller coaster. But we are not descending into a dictatorship. We are not heading towards another Civil War. And we are not watching our democratic institutions crumble.

Despite our great challenges, we are a vibrant, resilient and democratic nation. Still.

SEPTEMBER 15, 2020
WHY TRUMP WILL LEAVE OFFICE IF HE LOSES THE ELECTION

THERE is widespread concern that President Trump won't leave office if he loses the election. This angst is understandable. Trump has, after all, refused to affirmatively commit to a peaceful transfer of power.

But if Trump loses he will leave. Not, of course, because he wouldn't want to seize power and stay in office. But because he couldn't get away with it if he tried.

A fight about the election would ultimately go to the federal courts—just like it did in 2000. Trump won't stay in the White House if the courts rule against him. Why? Because staying would require Trump's entire administration, the military, and Congress—among others—to all conspire in violating two sacred principles of America's constitutional system: that courts are the final word in constitutional disputes and there are peaceful transitions of power after elections.

It won't happen.

There is broad recognition among liberals and conservatives alike that court orders must be followed. Always. Indeed, despite Trump's many losses in court—and despite his incendiary rhetoric criticizing the judiciary—he has not disobeyed a court order.

This principle began in 1803 with *Marbury v. Madison*, when Chief Justice John Marshall declared that it "is emphatically the duty of the Judicial Department to say what the law is." Ever since, federal courts have issued orders resolving disputes—and the rest of the government has obeyed and enforced them.

This was true when President Eisenhower sent federal troops into Arkansas to enforce the Supreme Court's decision in *Brown v. Board of Education*. It was true when the Supreme Court ordered President Nixon to hand over his incriminating oval office tapes. It was true when the Supreme Court decided the 2000 presidential election in favor of George W. Bush.

And it's true now.

Trump's Attorney General William Barr recently embraced this principle. Barr was asked: "Should the Supreme Court have the exclusive power to interpret the Constitution?" His response: "Yes." If Trump "believes that he has the power to do something under the Constitution," Barr continued, "he should be able to exercise that power. And if the Court disagrees and orders him not to, then he's lost the case."

And last week a unanimous Senate passed a resolution reaffirming its commitment to a peaceful transfer of the executive power.

True, Donald Trump has probably never heard of *Marbury v. Madison*. His allies are prone to making false statements. And he would happily disregard the courts to stay in office. But it's not up to him. It's up to the innumerable executive branch, military and congressional leaders who must legitimize his presidency and carry out his orders. As we learned from the Mueller report, Trump couldn't get his own White House counsel to fire Special Counsel Robert Mueller; he's not going to get his entire administration to seize the government.

Indeed, seizing power would be exponentially worse than anything Trump has attempted. It would be akin to signing and spending the annual budget without Congress's approval; refusing to recognize or participate in an impeachment process; or issuing an executive order firing a life-tenured Supreme Court Justice.

We should expect a partisan battle over the election. We should expect Trump to fight hard in the courts. We should expect tense moments. Surprises. Disappointments. Shocks. But, ultimately, Trump will not defy a court order and prevent the timely inauguration of Joe Biden.

Not because he wouldn't want to. But because he can't.

SEPTEMBER 19, 2020
TRUMP TARGETS TWITTER

PRESIDENT Trump's actions during his recent feud with Twitter were as Trumpian as it gets. Loud. Vindictive. And, ultimately, ineffective.

It started when Trump tweeted that mail-in ballots were "fraudulent" and California's plan to use them in November would cause a "Rigged Election."

Next, Twitter fact-checked Trump, adding a link to his tweets that invites people to "get the facts" about California's mail-in ballot program. Twitter's fact-check page states that "fact-checkers say there is no evidence that mail-in ballots are linked to voter fraud."

Finally, Trump signed an executive order calling for Section 230 of the Communications Decency Act to be "clarified" to limit liability immunity for online platforms like Twitter.

Beneath the bluster and haste, however, is a substantive legal document with broad ambitions but a limited likelihood of being consequential. The order requires federal agencies to take several steps.

First, the Federal Communications Commission must draft regulations clarifying that Section 230 provides no immunity to internet platforms that do not publish content in "good faith." The regulations are to require FCC staff to scrutinize whether platforms publish content in a "deceptive" way or without "reasoned" explanation of publishing decisions.

Second, the Office of Management and Budget must track how much federal agencies spend with online platforms. The Commerce Department, for example, spends large sums on U.S. census-related online advertising. The Department of Justice, in turn, must determine whether any internet platforms "are problematic vehicles for government speech due to viewpoint discrimination, deception to consumers, or other bad practices."

Finally, the order requires a series of additional steps including directing the Federal Trade Commission to search for unfair or deceptive acts, the Attorney General to create a working enforcement group with state attorneys general and the DOJ to prepare proposed federal legislation.

What does all this legalese amount to? Nothing, yet. It's one thing to actually change Section 230 by passing legislation. That would be significant. But it's quite another to simply order a bunch of bureaucrats to initiate projects.

Indeed, given the slow and dysfunctional workings of the administrative state—and the fact that there may soon be a new president who stops the initiative in its tracks—the order may have little consequence. On the other hand, though, the order's implementation could gain traction in a second Trump term and accelerate a growing push to regulate online platforms.

Add this to the list of reasons why November's presidential election is monumental.

What is known now is that Trump issuing this executive order fits within a recognizable pattern. First, he commits some high-profile impropriety. An involved party then responds. Next Trump lashes back at that party using the tools and platforms of his office—only, finally, to be slowed and stymied by the realities and frictions of governmental sausage making.

A more thoughtful and effective president would have started long ago preparing legislation to change Section 230. Trump's latest spasm could very well be too little, too late. Indeed, while Twitter's fact checking won't prevent Trump from continuing to speak loudly, he will still—compared to other presidents—carry a small stick.

SEPTEMBER 25, 2020
WHAT GINSBURG'S DEATH MEANS FOR THE 2020 PRESIDENTIAL ELECTION

Ruth Bader Ginsburg was perhaps the most consequential attorney in American history. As an advocate, she transformed the landscape for womens' rights. And, as a Justice on the Supreme Court, she authored numerous groundbreaking opinions.

Her recent death may also be immensely consequential: Her departure from the Supreme Court might change the winner of the 2020 presidential election from Joe Biden to Donald Trump.

The 2020 election may be decided by the Supreme Court—just like it was in 2000, when Ginsburg and her liberal colleagues dissented from the conservative majority's ruling handing George W. Bush the presidency. Indeed, both sides are already lining up armies of lawyers to fight over ballots in battleground states.

With Ginsburg on the Court, the main swing vote among the nine justices was John Roberts, the Chief Justice. Roberts has publicly clashed with Trump and ruled against him and his administration repeatedly. Most recently, Roberts wrote an opinion authorizing a New York state prosecutor to seek Trump's personal financial records.

Until Ginsburg is replaced, any 4-4 split decision among the eight justices will simply reaffirm the lower-appellate-court decision, whatever that may be. But if the Republicans confirm a new justice before the election—which is certainly their aim—John Roberts will no longer be the primary swing vote. Staunch conservatives Samuel Alito and Clarence Thomas will be aligned with Trump's three conservative appointees— Neil Gorsuch, Brett Kavanaugh and Ginsburg's replacement.

This would give the court a conservative majority, *even if Roberts were to rule against Trump.*

Put simply: Friday's seismic event doesn't just give Trump the opportunity to appoint another justice who will issue conservative rulings for decades to come. It gives Trump the opportunity to install a fifth vote in the potential Supreme Court battle for the United States presidency.

As we learned in *Bush v. Gore*, litigation over presidential elections has myriad complexities—ranging from issues of federalism and states' rights, to equal protection under the law—and therefore, if the election is close, the justices will have a menu of options to achieve the political result they desire. The near-term opportunity to confirm a conservative justice before November will be front and center for Trump and Republican Senate Majority Leader Mitch McConnell as they begin the process of replacing Ginsburg.

True, Senate Democrats will fiercely contest any Republican nomination. Perhaps additional Senate Republicans will join Susan Collins and Lisa Murkowski and support pushing off any confirmation vote until after the election. And the election may be sufficiently one-sided that the courts do not play a decisive role.

But this scenario—that Ginsburg's death flips the election from Biden to Trump—is no strained hypothetical. It is a concrete and plausible scenario.

The high drama surrounding the 2020 presidential election has officially begun.

OCTOBER 2, 2020
DONALD TRUMP IS NOT A DICTATOR

THERE are plenty of things for Americans to be concerned about right now. The coronavirus. Election interference. China. To name a few. But Donald Trump becoming a dictator is not one of them.

Many disagree. Journalist Jonathan Greenberg, for example, warned about the "twelve signs Trump would try to run a fascist dictatorship in his second term." National columnist Ann McFeatters explained that "I know authoritarianism when I see it. And that's what we've got in the good ol' USA." The Chairman of the House Judiciary Committee, Jerry Nadler, put it bluntly on the Senate floor during Trump's impeachment trial: "He is a dictator."

And so on.

These assertions stem from legitimate concerns about the 45th president. And Trump deserves much of the criticism he receives. But the narrative is confused.

Trump is no dictator.

For starters, the checks and balances in America's constitutional system won't let it happen. Indeed, federal and state governments consistently block Trump from achieving his goals. A Democrat-led Congress thwarted his legislative agenda and impeached him. The courts repeatedly rule against him and he has not once contested the legitimacy of those decisions. His own executive branch has investigated him for years and sent several of his associates to jail.

It is no different at the state level. Governors fight him

tooth and nail. Attorneys general sue him left and right. Even mayors contest his orders regularly. Trump is, moreover, loudly criticized by the press around the clock. His former allies and family members blast him in bestselling books. These things don't happen to dictators—who, by definition, significantly control their own government, press and people.

True, the rest of the government and the press can't make Trump more competent. Nor can they force him to stop tweeting absurdities—a pathological addiction that stains and undermines his presidency. And Trump, like all presidents, has wide latitude to act in foreign affairs. (Foreign policy miscalculation, not domestic concentration of power, is the true danger of the Trump presidency.)

These are all important, and concerning, limitations on the ability to restrain Trump. But that does not make him an all-powerful dictator.

Indeed, the Supreme Court—in a resounding rejection of this narrative—allowed a state prosecutor to seek Trump's personal financial information. Is there anything less dictatorial than the head of state being subject to criminal process by the local prosecutor?

The second reason why the narrative that Trump is a dictator is confused is because he doesn't have the talent, understanding or focus to seize dictatorial control over the entire nation. Being a dictator is not easy. Even if you inherit it from your father (like Kim Jong-un) or seize it from the ashes of a disintegrated empire (like Vladimir Putin), maintaining dictatorship over an entire nation is a hard business.

Trump is simply not up to the task. He does not understand

the United States government well enough to seize it. Trump is the most constitutionally illiterate president in our history. Recall, for example, his claim that his "authority" over states "is total" in addressing the coronavirus—an absurdity (scoffed at by governors and mayors alike) that conflicts with elemental principles of federalism.

If anything, in the zero-sum power struggle between the various factions of government, Trump is losing ground to more effective participants at both the federal and state level.

Donald Trump (like all presidents) is very powerful. His presidency is a challenge to the republic in numerous ways. He is, to be sure, a braggart, a bully, a danger. And so on.

But a dictator? Not even close.

6/ THE CRIMINALIZATION OF POLITICS

"There is no greater tyranny than that which is perpetrated under the shield of the law and in the name of justice."

—*Charles de Montesquieu*

ONE of the most concerning parts of the American stress test is the ever-increasing criminalization of politics. Respect for the rule of law—a core principle of American democracy—requires that the criminal-justice system not impact people unevenly based on their politics. This is not just about courtesy or fairness to politicians. Criminalizing politics creates dysfunction at the center of government, handicapping those in office and deterring others from serving the public.

It is one thing to even-handedly enforce the law and prosecute clear violations of existing crimes. This is necessary to maintain civil society. And it applies to politicians just like to everyone else. But it's quite another to painstakingly search for political opponents' legal violations and apply novel and aggressive interpretations of the law to entrap and incriminate them. The latter has been a daily part of American politics in the Trump era.

In January, 2022, for example, former Republican Speaker of the House of Representatives Newt Gingrich raised the specter of jail time for members of Congress who were investigating the events surrounding the January 6, 2021 riot at the United States Capitol. "I think when you have a Republican Congress, this is all going to come crashing down," Gingrich told Fox News. "And the wolves are going to find out that they're now sheep and they're the ones who are in fact, I think, facing a real risk of jail for the kinds of laws they're breaking."

Republican member of the January 6 committee Liz Cheney aptly responded: "A former Speaker of the House is threatening jail time for members of Congress who are investigating the violent January 6 attack on our Capitol and our Constitution," Cheney said on her Twitter account. "This is what it looks like when the rule of law unravels."

In a healthy democracy political differences are resolved at the ballot box; in failed states they are resolved in criminal court rooms. As the columns that follow illustrate, America is backsliding along this continuum.

OCTOBER 10, 2020
THE CRIMINALIZATION OF POLITICS

Aᴍᴇʀɪᴄᴀɴ politics has become criminalized. A steady drum beat of words and deeds—from chanting "lock her up," to prosecuting President Trump's associates, to Trump pushing for Joe Biden's indictment—has eroded the bright line between politics and the criminal law.

This is deeply troubling for several reasons.

First, criminalizing politics conflicts with the bedrock principle that the rule of law applies equally to all people. Entangling the passions of politics with the criminal law leads to treating people differently based on their political affiliation, instead of on their guilt or innocence. This is antithetical to even-handed justice.

The examples of this criminalization are endless. Republicans want to lock up Hillary Clinton for her email practices and prosecute Obama administration officials for investigating the Trump campaign. Democrats, meanwhile, want Michael Flynn in prison and Trump indicted in New York the day he leaves office. And so on.

In American politics the messenger matters more than the message, the actor matters more than the act. This is diametrically opposed to the basic premise of the rule of law—that all people must be treated equally and their specific alleged misdeeds are what matter.

Second, criminalizing politics accelerates a disturbing trend towards ever more political polarization. It ramps up the stakes from treating opponents like political rivals to treating them like sworn enemies.

True, fierce domestic politics is nothing new. It is woven into the fabric of our democratic system. But ultimately we are one nation in a dangerous world. Our political disputes should not consume a disproportionate amount of our national bandwidth. Nor should they undercut our ability to respond to the many foreign threats we face. If looked at from a global perspective, Americans' interests overlap far more than they diverge.

Put simply, Americans should focus their political energy on winning elections and setting the right policies, not sending officials they don't like to jail.

Finally, criminalizing politics deters talented people from entering the political arena. The United States government already has a personnel problem. Americans shouldn't further dissuade quality people from entering government because imperfections or ambiguities in their past might be shoehorned into politically motivated criminal accusations. The downside for winning office should be losing the next election, not getting indicted.

These concerns about the criminalization of politics must be looked at in context. It is of course true that entering the government should neither absolve someone from past crimes nor serve as a license to commit new ones. And one aspect of even-handed justice is to prosecute not just the weak and anonymous but also the powerful and well known.

Striking the right balance is hard. But there should be a strong presumption in favor of leaving politics—and its inherent passions and prejudices—at the courthouse door. Criminalizing politics doesn't just poison our government and undermine our justice system. It imperils our nation as a whole.

OCTOBER 22, 2020
PROSECUTORIAL DISCRETION IN PARTISAN TIMES

MANY of the same people who criticized Attorney General William Barr for showing leniency towards Roger Stone and Michael Flynn in their criminal matters are now calling for Joe Biden to prosecute President Trump if Biden wins the presidency.

This raises two questions fundamental to our legal system: Who in the federal government decides whether to prosecute alleged wrong-doers? And what criteria frames this analysis?

The answer to the first question is easy: Federal prosecutors. The awesome power to take another citizen's liberty is wielded by those at the Department of Justice. A civilized society must have a criminal-justice system, which depends on prosecutors bringing cases. While this is an enormous responsibility to vest in individuals who are largely untethered from democratic processes, there is no real alternative.

The key question, then, is the second one: What criteria frames—and restrains—the decision-making regarding whether to bring a case?

The discomforting answer is that prosecutorial discretion is primarily a matter of subjective human judgment. And human judgment in this context is just as ridden with bias and fallibility as in any other. The principle bias impacting prosecutorial discretion is confirmation bias—the strong propensity in human thinking to interpret new facts as consistent with existing beliefs.

Prosecutors, of course, are a heterogeneous group and

this bias impacts every prosecutor differently. Most prosecutors are well-intentioned and loyal public servants. But, as humans, they often interpret new facts uncovered during investigations as consistent with their preconceived notions and prejudices. In the arena of criminal justice—where life and liberty are at stake—this bias can have dramatic human consequences, especially when the target of an investigation is a controversial public figure.

Bias in prosecutorial decision-making is, moreover, fundamentally at odds with the first principle of criminal justice—that the law applies equally to all individuals. America has a long and scurrilous history of enforcing the criminal law one way towards favored groups and another towards disfavored groups. The Jim Crow system had explicitly racist laws on the books. But a law, alone, does little harm. The real damage was done by the unwritten biases of the prosecutors who chose which defendants to pursue. Disparate results still exist today. Of the two-plus million American inmates a staggering disproportion are minorities. The biases and prejudices of the people who bring the cases impact this disparity.

Prosecutorial discretion is, indeed, an immense power. Unlike other decisions in our democracy that require an election among the people or a majority vote of elected representatives, deciding whether to prosecute someone comes down to individual human judgment, largely unobserved and unchecked. As former Attorney General and Supreme Court Justice Robert Jackson said, "The prosecutor has more control over life, liberty, and reputation than any other person in America. His discretion is tremendous."

Different people looking at the same set of facts often come to radically different conclusions. And it's no different with lawyers. Whether someone is prosecuted or not thus often boils down to the luck of the draw—to which prosecutor happens to be on the case.

Many of the people calling for Trump's prosecution have long been proponents of criminal-justice reform and reining in unfettered prosecutorial discretion. Sure, they say, the legal system is flawed; so only "clear crimes" committed by Trump should be prosecuted. But what, exactly, is a clear crime? In the House of Representatives, 100 percent of Democrats found Trump committed an impeachable offense (a constitutional "high crime") and 100 percent of Republicans found that he did not. Identifying a clear crime is not that simple, especially when the visceral prejudices of politics are involved.

There will never be an algorithm that determines—yes or no—whether someone should be prosecuted. And, yet, we depend upon prosecutors bringing cases, including against politicians, to deter criminal behavior and keep society functioning.

Striking the right balance is difficult, complicated—and essential.

So how, then, should a prosecutor (or anyone else) conclude whether another citizen's liberty should be jeopardized by a prosecution? With profound caution. And this requires a decent respect for the inherent biases in human judgment. Even—indeed, especially—when the potential defendant is a political opponent.

NOVEMBER 2, 2020
IN DEFENSE OF (GASP) WILLIAM BARR
AND ROGER STONE

ALL criminal defendants are entitled to the basic protections of criminal procedure and due process and should not be subject to excessive punishment.

This includes Roger Stone—a controversial and often-criticized political operative.

Indeed, the more there exists pre-existing animus toward the defendant—no matter what side of the political aisle she or he may reside—the more important it is to safeguard the defendant from improper prosecutions or disproportionate sentences. Why? Because the use of state coercion to deprive a citizen of her or his liberty is (other than the ability to wage war) the most dangerous power vested in government. It must be exercised with extreme caution.

Always.

In February, the Department of Justice withdrew its nine-year sentencing recommendation for Stone after President Trump criticized the recommendation in a tweet. This created quite a stir in Washington and the media, with many outraged by the DOJ's abrupt change.

During Attorney General William Barr's recent visit to the House Judiciary Committee, it was clear that Democrats are still rankled. In response to accusations of favoritism towards a Trump associate, Barr explained why he lowered the recommendation. "The line prosecutors were trying to advocate for a sentence that was more than twice what anyone else in a similar position had ever served, and this is a 68-year-old man, first-time offender and no violence," he said. "I agree the president's friends don't deserve special breaks, but they also don't deserve to be treated more harshly than other people."

Barr is wrong about plenty of things, but he's right about this. Equal justice requires that all people—whether Trump friend or foe—are treated the same under the law.

Why would Stone, a nonviolent offender, deserve a punishment more than twice as severe as any other similarly situated defendant? Because he's friends with Trump? Because he plays dirty politics? Those considerations simply can't infect the decision-making when someone's liberty is at stake. Indeed, Stone is a 68-year-old man who might not survive nine years in prison. The prosecutors' recommended sentence is thus the rough equivalent of seeking the death penalty.

Moreover, as detailed in multiple inspector-general reports, the investigation into Trump's ties with Russia which led to Stone's prosecution was started under questionable conditions that included law-enforcement officials making material misrepresentations to the Foreign Intelligence Surveillance Court. And after a yearslong investigation into Stone, Special Counsel Robert Mueller's team did not find evidence establishing that Stone colluded with Russia to hack into the Democratic National Committee's email servers. Instead, after prosecutors determined that Stone did not commit this alleged underlying crime, but rather may have interfered with Mueller's investigation, a large team of armed law-enforcement officials went to

Stone's house—along with CNN cameras—and arrested him and took him to jail. Stone was eventually convicted of committing these crimes, seven counts in all. It was the first time he was ever convicted of a crime.

This background is brushed aside by those incensed—*still*—that Barr would withdraw the sentencing recommendation after Trump's tweets.

Yes, as Barr has explained, Trump should abstain from interfering with or publicly weighing in regarding the particulars of any DOJ criminal case, including Stone's. And this is important. Trump's shattering of norms with respect to the DOJ has been reckless and disturbing. But do Trump's actions mean that someone else—Roger Stone—should serve more time than he otherwise deserves? Of course not. And does the fact that Barr's lowering of Stone's sentencing recommendation was unusual mean that it was the wrong thing to do? Not at all. Far better to deviate from the norm to get to the right decision about someone's liberty than to myopically stick with past practice. Administering even-handed justice—not blindly maintaining departmental continuity—is the DOJ's lodestar.

Changing the excessive sentencing recommendation, under these background circumstances, was a humane approach to law enforcement. Notwithstanding Trump's improper tweets (and the long-lasting anger of Barr's critics) it was the right thing to do.

The judge, who later sentenced Stone to just over three years, agrees.

7/ ELECTION SEASON

"Rage and phrenzy will pull down more in half an hour, than prudence, deliberation, and foresight can build up in a hundred years."

—*Edmund Burke*

DONALD Trump's activity surrounding the 2020 presidential election—before, during, and after—was the worst behavior of any sitting president in American history. Before the election, Trump (watching the polls tilt towards Democratic nominee Joe Biden) claimed that mail-in voting would generate fraud in Biden's favor. "The ballots are out of control … You know it. And you know who knows it better than anybody else? The Democrats know it better than anybody else." Mail-in ballots, Trump said, are "a whole big scam."

Biden won the election. On cue, Trump implemented his game plan by promulgating the "Big Lie," a series of baseless assertions that widespread fraud gave Biden the presidency. For example, at a December rally before Georgia's run-off Senatorial elections, Trump said, "They cheated and they rigged our presidential election, and they're gonna try to rig this election too."

There was, however, no evidence of widespread election fraud. Zero. As Dave Wasserman of the nonpartisan Cook Political Report put it, "The case for Trump having won the election is so preposterous that the only explanation is that the losing side does not like the results." Trump nonetheless filed dozens of lawsuits trying to reverse the results. He lost every time. The claims were so weak his lawyers now face sanctions and debarment for bringing them. In America's three-branch system of government the courts resolve disputes and this uniform procession of lopsided defeats conclusively established that Trump's claims were baseless.

He didn't care. The Big Lie grew bigger: "NO WAY WE LOST THIS ELECTION!" he tweeted weeks after the election.

American democracy depends as its basic premise on the sanctity of its elections. It is the highest duty of elected officials to instill faith in our electoral processes, so the people trust democracy is working—and therefore respect and legitimize the workings of government and the rule of law. Trust in elections is thus not just one ingredient in a democracy, it is a necessary precondition to consensual government.

Donald Trump blatantly—with malice aforethought—sought not just to undermine America's electoral system but to vacate it. He tried to reverse the results of the presidential election, while claiming *he* was the victim of the fraud. Had he succeeded American democracy would have existed in theory only.

Trump's post-election behavior was so disturbing that on January 3, 2021 all living former United States Secretaries of Defense warned Trump against using the military in the election dispute: "Efforts to involve the u.s. armed forces in resolving election disputes would take us into dangerous, unlawful and unconstitutional territory. Civilian and military officials who direct or carry out such measures would be accountable, including potentially facing criminal penalties, for the grave consequences of their actions on our republic."

The stress test climaxed three days later on January 06, 2021. Trump held a rally several blocks from the United States Capitol as Congress was certifying the presidential election. He said to the crowd: "We're going to walk down to the Capitol, and we're going to cheer on our brave senators and congressmen and women, and we're probably not going to be cheering so much for some of them, because you'll never take back our country with weakness. You have to show strength, and you have to be strong." Trump also said that "I know that everyone here will soon be marching over to the Capitol building to peacefully and patriotically make your voices heard."

His supporters then stormed the Capitol and ransacked the building. Several people died. The election-certification proceedings stopped. The American stress test—before then a war of ideas—exploded into the physical realm as Trump's mob halted essential government proceedings with force and violence.

As the rioters breached the Capitol, Vice President Mike Pence was participating in the election-certification proceedings. Trump wanted him to try to overturn the results. Pence refused. As the salivating mob roamed the Capitol, looking for Pence, Trump tweeted: "Mike Pence didn't have the courage to do what should have been done to protect our Country and our Constitution."

In both symbolism and substance, it was one of the worst events in American history. Yet again Donald Trump had turned the inconceivable into reality in all the wrong ways. As the columns in this chapter illustrate, America is still reeling from the aftermath of that day.

JANUARY 15, 2021
THE WAY FORWARD

Donald Trump's America has plunged below rock bottom. The coronavirus has taken hundreds of thousands of lives. Trump has spent years debasing America's foundational institutions—while being cheered on wildly by half the country. And Congress was assaulted, by a violent mob, while carrying out the most essential democratic function of all: the peaceful transfer of power after an election.

Where do we go from here?

America must achieve two objectives to reverse the spiraling trend line and restore its sanity and stability.

First, America must reduce its political divisiveness. The polarized rot at the extremes of America's polity are rapidly gaining market share. And the common way to address divisiveness—insisting that the other side is bad and must change—has only deepened the divide. The antidote to polarization is not uncompromising demands (however eloquent or well-reasoned) that one's political opponents roll over.

Instead, the way forward is to finally start compromising—to give the other side concrete policy wins when possible. This, in turn, lessens the sting of their own concessions, thereby spinning the political flywheel in the right direction.

Of course, politics will always be a partisan enterprise. Electoral winners shouldn't be expected to embrace policies antithetical to their fundamental values. And large coalitions on both sides are unlikely to budge. But, in Trump's after-math, moderates on both sides must become first-movers in a substantive shift towards bipartisanship. The alternative is more of the same: an ever-accelerating descent into political madness.

The second thing Americans must do to restore national stability is resist the urge to overreact to Trump's presidency. Perhaps the one thing all Americans can agree on is that Donald Trump is an outlier. The Biden presidency is a sharp reversion to the mean, a restoration to normality and sanity in the executive branch.

The rules and institutions of American government should be engineered to withstand an anomaly like Donald Trump. But they should not be premised on Trump becoming the norm. We should not overreact and, for example, elim-inate core free speech for Trump's allies, reshape executive power in response to Trump's abuses, or pursue overzealous prosecutions of Trump's friends.

In response to Watergate, Congress passed the 1978 Independent Counsel Act—a misguided and constitution-ally dubious overreaction to Richard Nixon's presidency. The mistake came into sharp focus as Ken Starr brazenly investigated Bill Clinton. And after Clinton's impeach-ment the Department of Justice corrected the error by rewriting the rules for appointing independent prosecutors. We shouldn't make similar mistakes now.

These two objectives, reducing divisiveness and not over-reacting to Trump, go hand in hand. They are rooted not just in reverence for America's history but confidence that our constitutional system works as designed.

Abraham Lincoln asked at Gettysburg whether this nation could long endure. And it has. Lincoln's sweeping pardon of all Confederate soldiers after the Civil War reverberates today. Instead of punishing the soldiers, Lincoln forgave them. And he trusted that America's constitutional system could harness the potential of all Americans, not simply his political allies. What followed was the most successful national reemergence in history.

Lincoln understood that after years of violence and division the key ingredients for restoring American stability were compromise with his adversaries and confidence in the essential principles of American government.

The same is true now.

FEBRUARY 25, 2021
THE SENATE MUST CONVICT AND DISQUALIFY DONALD TRUMP

AFTER months of hyping conspiracy theories and pressuring election officials to falsify results, Donald Trump incited a mob to storm the United States Capitol and stop Congress from certifying the presidential election. While Trump's critics have often overstated their case against him, their condemnation of his actions after the election are, finally, proportional to Trump's offenses. If his acts do not warrant conviction in his upcoming Senate trial, what possibly could?

The Senate must convict Trump and disqualify him from ever holding office again.

First, Trump's actions easily qualify as an impeachable offense. The Senate may convict and disqualify Trump if he committed "treason, bribery, or other high crimes and misdemeanors" under the United States Constitution. The key question, then, is whether Trump committed a high crime or misdemeanor.

Of course he did. Trump may not have known the mob would physically breach the capital. And he may not have wanted five people to die as a result. But he organized and incited his supporters to physically halt Congressional proceedings.

This is not just a crime; and it's not just a high crime. Trump tried to violate the most essential principle in American democracy: that the peaceful transfer of power follows an election. This principle is, indeed, the basic necessity on which the rest of our democratic system rests. The alternative to the peaceful transfer of power—the usurpation of power by an incumbent against the will of the people—is the antithesis of democracy.

Second, the Senate may convict and disqualify Trump even though he left office. The text of the Constitution doesn't limit impeachment to incumbent presidents. As then-former president John Quincy Adams said while sitting in the House of Representatives: "I hold myself, so long as I have the breath of life in my body, amenable to impeachment by this House for everything I did during the time I held any public office." And there are numerous examples in both American and British law of officials being impeached after leaving office.

Of course, if the contrary were true—and a president could escape a Senate trial by resigning or committing crimes just before leaving office—then the Constitution's disqualification remedy would be hollow. And, ultimately, the Senate resolves open constitutional questions, like this one, about its own proceedings.

Finally, Trump's efforts to overturn the election conclusively establish he is unfit to be president. The debate about that is over. A presidential election is the ultimate source of legitimacy in our democracy. It is the only time all Americans come together and vote on the same question. This legitimacy weighed in Trump's favor for years—protecting him against widespread efforts to remove him from office—even though his behavior was consistently disturbing. The people had spoken in 2016; and they had elected Donald Trump.

Yet this same essential consideration—that presidential elections are the deepest reflection of the people's will that our system affords—led to Trump's catastrophic demise when he tried to reverse Joe Biden's victory.

The Constitution provides enormous leeway for presidential misbehavior. It is not an impeachable offense to be crass, inappropriate, immoral, irrational, even reckless. But the Constitution likewise has foundational rules that presidents must follow. For months, Trump was at war with the most fundamental one of all, the peaceful transfer of power. And this culminated in his incitement of the mob that sought, through violence, to overturn the presidential election.

Donald Trump's behavior was an offense—a constitutional high crime—unlike any other in our nation's history. He must never hold office again.

MAY 15, 2021
STATES CAN STILL BAN TRUMP FROM THE BALLOT IN 2024

THE United States Senate acquitted Donald Trump after his impeachment trial. Again. The Democrats' aim, this time, was to disqualify Trump from running for president in 2024.

But the acquittal doesn't necessarily mean that Trump can be president a second time. While the Senate has the authority to convict and disqualify Trump after he is impeached, the states have a say in the matter, too.

Section 3 of the 14th Amendment to the United States Constitution prevents federal officials from holding office again who have "engaged in insurrection" against the United States. Trump's actions before and on January 6, 2021—when he incited a deadly mob to assault the United States Capitol—may qualify as insurrection under Section 3.

This means that individual states, which handle their own electoral processes, can decide whether Trump should be on the ballot. While Congress can pass legislation asserting that Trump violated Section 3, the controversy would not be concrete—and thus subject to final judicial resolution—until states actually ban Trump from the ballot. If enough states did so, the effort could effectively prevent Trump from winning.

If Trump does run, and numerous states ban him, the resulting litigation would eventually reach the United States Supreme Court. The question before the Justices would be whether Trump's actions amounted to insurrection under Section 3. Instead of a surface-level political fight resolved largely along party lines, as we saw in the Senate, the Supreme Court would render a reasoned constitutional determination. Its decision, moreover, would be based on a fully developed factual record—unlike the thin record before the Senate. (We will learn a lot about what happened before and on January 6th in the coming four years.)

So what, then, would the Supreme Court ultimately decide?

With four years of Joe Biden as president—and perhaps a different composition of Justices as a result—the Supreme Court just might bar Trump from running. We already know the conservative Justices are not afraid to rule against Trump in major election cases. Indeed, they uniformly rejected Trump's efforts to litigate the 2020 presidential election results.

The prospect that Trump gets banned from the ballot in 2024, moreover, has practical implications now. It should deter reasonable Republicans from supporting Trump in the first place: Such a risky candidate is not a winning horse. And the threat of litigating whether Trump committed insurrection—and the intense scrutiny on his actions such litigation would bring—may, itself, deter Trump from reentering the fray.

Donald Trump incited a mob to storm the United States Capitol to prevent the peaceful transfer of executive power. Despite the gravity of this offense, Senate Republicans did not disqualify him from holding office again. The Supreme Court, however, might not be so forgiving.

8/ THE BIG PICTURE

"It is not the function of our government to keep the citizen from falling into error; it is the function of the citizen to keep the government from falling into error."

—*Robert H. Jackson*

Aמ. ERICAN democracy survived the Trump presidency. But Trump's troubles—and the corresponding troubles for the country—continue.

As a civilian Trump no longer enjoys the legal protections of the presidency, including immunity from indictment. He's being broadly investigated. The Department of Justice and Congress are investigating the events surrounding the January 6, 2021 Capitol riot. Congress released notes taken by then-Deputy Attorney General Richard Donoghue revealing Trump's attempt to pressure then-Acting Attorney General Jeffrey Rosen into saying the election was corrupt: "Just say the election was corrupt and leave the rest to me," Trump told Rosen in late 2020.

In New York, Trump's company and its Chief Financial Officer have been indicted. The charges allege that the Trump Organization kept two sets of books: one for lenders (showing rosy financials to attract good financing terms) and one for the tax authorities (showing lousy financials to reduce tax liability). The indictment also alleges the Trump Organization evaded millions of dollars in taxes by paying secret bonuses to employees. Separate New York prosecutors also announced in October 2021 an investigation into the finances of Trump's New York golf course. And the New York Attorney General's office is broadly investigating Trump and his family's business dealings.

In Georgia, Trump is under criminal investigation for his activities after the 2020 presidential election. As part of Trump's broad campaign to overturn the election results, he pressured local election officials to reverse the results and "find 11,780 votes." From a legal perspective this may be more troubling than his speech on January 6, 2021, when he spoke in a public forum with First Amendment protections. In Georgia, by contrast, Trump tried to intimidate officials into committing election fraud while outside of public view.

Moreover, Trump's friends Tom Barrack, Rudy Giuliani, Roger Stone and Steve Bannon are all reportedly under criminal investigation. None of them are necessarily above turning on Trump in exchange for leniency. And Trump, of course, can no longer dangle presidential pardons from the Oval Office in exchange for loyalty.

Trump has initiated several lawsuits, too. In July 2021, he sued Twitter, YouTube and Facebook for banning him from their platforms. Trump's legal theory, clumsily articulated in the complaint, is that these social networks act on behalf of the government and therefore the First Amendment prohibits them from blocking his speech. He also sued the New York Times and his niece Mary Trump for publicly disclosing his confidential tax information. And in March 2022 he sued Hillary Clinton, James Comey, the Democratic National Committee and others, levying broad and indiscriminate accusations relating to the government's investigation into the Trump campaign's ties with Russia.

Meanwhile Trump keeps on lying about the election. "We were doing so well until the rigged election happened to come along," he told the Conservative Political Action Conference (CPAC) in July 2021. "This was an election where the person that counts the votes was far more important than the candidate," he continued to a raucous, adoring crowd. "They failed to call out the late night ballot stuffing that took place in Georgia."

By early 2022 Trump had amassed a $122 million political war chest. Despite the tumult and damage of his four years in office, he is still a dominant force in American politics.

The columns that follow take a bird's-eye view of American democracy—where it's been; where it's heading— as the Trump-era stress test continues on.

JULY 5, 2021
AMERICA FIRST, LAST AND ONLY

COVID-19 is still wreaking havoc globally. Cases in Africa are rising sharply. Hospital systems in many countries, including Nepal, Iran, Bangladesh and Sri Lanka, have been overwhelmed. And Japan—currently in a state of emergency—may postpone this summer's Tokyo Olympics. This year the world will far exceed last year's 1.8 million Covid-19 deaths.

Yet things are improving in America. Indeed, to many Americans the pandemic is disappearing. New York Times columnist Paul Krugman recently celebrated "extraordinary good news: The virus is losing, and the economy is winning."

The contrast is striking: A pandemic that many Americans think is in the rearview mirror is still front and center in many countries.

These disparate circumstances are hardly new. As America's GDP has soared past $65,000 per person, over a billion people elsewhere still live in poverty. And the economic impact of Covid-19 on developing nations has been staggering. As America's economy roars back to growth the World Bank estimates that up to 150 million people will fall into extreme poverty because of the pandemic.

America—yet again—finds itself much better off than most of the world.

What's different now, however, is that because of Covid-19 America's well-being directly hinges on the well-being of others. This is true not just in the usual, attenuated ways (like reducing the cost of goods through global trade) but through the direct life-and-death connection of a pandemic. Indeed, as the virus rages globally the risk of vaccine-proof mutations reaching America's shores increases proportionally.

Like it or not, humanity is in it together.

Perhaps this interconnected fate will diminish one of the worst aspects of America's national character: a chilling indifference to the rest of the world. Americans tend to focus on themselves, on their families, on their communities, on those in their own political, socioeconomic or religious tribes. Their problems tend to be local problems. They fixate on up-close concerns.

Indeed, a more accurate slogan than Donald Trump's "America First" would be "America First, Last and Only." America is selfish when it comes to international aid; its contribution is less than one percent of the federal budget. Its politics are dominated by domestic concerns; Americans are currently haggling over how many trillions to spend on themselves. And millions of Americans want to build ever-larger barriers at the nation's southern border; many even want to rescind the Deferred Action for Childhood Arrivals program (DACA) and ship talented American-born kids out of the country.

Part of why Americans have been so self-absorbed is because they could always get away with it. But not now. Not with a still-rampaging virus that respects no national boundary.

One positive that can emerge from the pandemic is that

America becomes a more empathetic nation on the global stage. The first ingredient in empathy is awareness of others: You can't value people whose lives are not on your radar. And the plight of people in less-fortunate nations is gaining increased visibility domestically as Covid-19's global wreckage fills America's own front pages.

Ideally, this newfound attention on others will foster a lasting concern for foreign nations. Going forward Americans should have a more inclusive view of who matters—embracing the principle that every human life has equal value irrespective of where someone was born or what someone looks like. America is a great nation. But it is not an empathetic one. It has prospered for centuries while maintaining an isolated indifference to the rest of the world. Covid-19 is changing that. America is looking more outward now, and other nations should remain in its field of vision after the pandemic subsides.

Is it understandable that, to many Americans, America should come first? Sure. But the people of other nations should matter, too.

AUGUST 25, 2021
POWER TO THE PEOPLE

FAMED columnist Walter Lipmann warned in 1925 about the dangers of too much democracy. Lipman argued that the American populace ("the bewildered herd") must not overly influence government policy. Instead of a true democracy, in which the people directly control the country, Lipman advocated for maintaining a protective intermediary of sophisticated elites—in politics, the press and business—lodged between the people and governmental power. This structure, according to Lipmann, would maintain stability and ensure rational policy making.

A century later, the election of Donald Trump lent credence to Lipmann's thesis. Trump's primary communication method as president was Twitter, an unfiltered channel connecting him directly to voters. Trump's election and presidency broadly disempowered elite intermediaries—including GOP party elders, global business leaders and mainstream media institutions—long accustomed to directly influencing American governance.

As Lipman predicted, it did not go well. Paradoxically, Trump's Twitter version of direct democracy sharply decreased the strength of democratic self-governance, culminating in Trump's Twitter-organized mob storming the United States Capitol as Congress tried to certify the 2020 presidential election.

This rise in democracy has only intensified in the five years since Trump was elected, as the intermediaries between power and the people continue to disintegrate.

Social media is the prime example. Platforms like Twitter, Facebook and Instagram allow politicians to bypass traditional media gatekeepers and communicate directly with voters. Anyone online can instantaneously publish their thoughts, with each tweet or post potentially reverberating around the globe. This personal empowerment has coincided with a rise in populism—and authoritarianism—around the world.

The revolution has disrupted finance, too. Take, for example, the extreme volatility of GameStop's stock. Driven by Reddit's online forums and Robinhood (which empowers people to effortlessly trade stocks without a middle-person collecting fees), GameStop's price per share has swung violently for many months. The gyrations have wiped out many small investors.

Even sports are being transformed. The Fan Controlled Football League, which debuted this year, allows fans to call the plays online—destroying the age-old barrier between the coach, who controlled the shots, and the fans who simply watched.

Are these democratic revolutions a good thing? Put another way, is civilization better off with sophisticated elites controlling the framework of society—or is it better having the people, unrestrained, barreling forward with the shackles thrown off?

The United States Constitution is a guide. While imperfect, the Constitution deftly harnesses the competing impulses between elite control and democratic rule. The founding fathers' solution: Strike a balance. On the one hand, the American people elect members of Congress and the president. At the same time, however, government power is consistently shielded from the governed: Judges have life-time appointments; the electoral college overrides the pop-ular vote; and the people have no direct legislative role.

A balanced approach likewise makes sense when con-fronting today's vexing problems. Everyone can have a Twitter account, but inciting violence must be prohibited. Everyone can trade stocks, but new forms of market manip-ulation must be strenuously regulated. And the marketplace for fan-controlled sports should be free to flourish alongside the traditional coach-controlled leagues.

Striking the right balance between elite influence and popular control is as complex as it is important. Yet it may become merely an academic subject. The trend line is clear: Lipman's intermediaries are dying on the vine. For better or worse, the future belongs to the herd.

OCTOBER 25, 2021
AMERICAN INCOMPETENCE

A<small>T</small> the turn of the 21st century America was a unipolar global power. A decade after winning the Cold War, it was an economic, political and military hegemon.

Just two decades later, China is a geopolitical rival, America can neither protect its people from a virus nor its critical infrastructure from a cyber hacker, and Donald Trump—fresh off the presidency—is at war with America's most essential democratic traditions.

The common thread tying together America's failures is dysfunctional and incompetent governance. The world's oldest and most successful constitutional democracy must take several steps to reverse the trend line.

First, America must re-embrace rational discourse. The American people—and therefore their elected officials—focus disproportionately on partisan triviality. Indeed, the latest salvo in the fight between Congresswomen Alexandria Ocasio-Cortez (D-N.Y) and Marjorie Taylor Greene (R-Ga)—however riveting—should not get more attention than the latest military developments in the South China Sea.

The culpability for this misfocus is widespread. Elected officials must moderate their rhetoric. Serious journalists must resist joining the partisan fray. And adult voters must exhibit maturity in the public square. The problem with squabbling over triviality is that it diverts energy and attention from what matters. And a lot does. America's international challenges are growing: In addition to a rising China, the governments of Iran, Russia, and North Korea remain dangerous adversaries; Covid-19 variants continue to emerge from across the globe; and supply-chain shortages and inflation threaten the global economy.

The bandwidth left over to address these problems—after the partisan brawling—is shrinking.

Second, America must pass effective, bipartisan legislation repairing its crumbling infrastructure. Soon. America needs a strong foundation to compete on the fiercely competitive global stage. In addition to rebuilding its roads, bridges and airports—a long-neglected national embarrassment—America must make the internet readily available to everyone. No country can prosper in a digital world with large groups of citizens offline. And the internet must be safe. America cannot withstand the bad intentions of cyber criminals—many of whom are rival nation states—if it does not dramatically bolster its cyber defenses. If current trends continue, the Colonial Pipeline ransomware attack will be the first chapter in an escalating story of cyber criminals attacking America's critical infrastructure.

Finally, America must reduce Donald Trump's influence. This is easier said than done, of course. But it could not be more essential. In an era of hysterical overstatements it is, if anything, an understatement to say that Trump is at war—expressly and unapologetically—with America's basic premise of consensual government. The peaceful transfer of power is, indeed, the touchstone of democracy. An election is meaningless if a corresponding restructuring of government does not follow. Trump's maniacal lying about the 2020 presidential election jeopardizes the public's trust in the election system, a prerequisite to its survival.

These three necessities—rationalizing discourse, strengthening infrastructure and marginalizing Donald Trump—go hand in hand. America cannot have competent leaders without rational voters. It cannot have effective legislation without sober-minded legislators. And it cannot function as a civil society if its loudest voice is uncivil and unhinged. The world is far too dangerous and complicated for the halls of American government to be mired in triviality, stasis and dysfunction.

After visiting America in the mid-19th century, French political philosopher Alexis de Tocqueville said that "the greatness of America lies not in being more enlightened than any other nation, but rather in her ability to repair her faults." We will find out, soon enough, whether this is still true.

9/   WHO WILL COUNT THE VOTES

"I consider it completely unimportant who in the party will vote, or how; but what is extraordinarily important is this—who will count the votes, and how."

—*attributed to Joseph Stalin*

Donald Trump has filled his post-presidency with back-ward-looking grievances about the 2020 presidential election. Well over a year after his loss at the polls, he still can't let it go. In March 2022, for example, Trump said that "the ballot harvesting scam will go down as the biggest political scandal in history. It is totally determinative, and the Democrats are doing everything they can to stop the news from coming out. Republicans must be strong and unified in order to save our Country."

This narrative was false when Trump started it just after the election. And it's false now.

As Trump's former Attorney General William Barr said in March 2022, "there was no stealing of the election through fraud. Which means, you know, that people who were not qualified to vote or didn't exist, their votes were counted, or good votes were subtracted. The votes reflected the decision of the people." The "evidence" that Trump cites, Barr continued, is "nonsense" and "just false."

But Trump's focus has been forward-looking, too. He is looking ahead, to 2024, for a potential presidential run. And he has homed in on perhaps the most sensitive vulnerability in American democracy: the people who count the votes. Trump is trying to get his diehard supporters installed to oversee the 2024 elections in battleground states.

As a result of Trump's relentless focus on vote counting, Americans' trust in elections is falling. Take, for example, two polls conducted by CNN. In January 2021, 59% of people polled were either "very" or "somewhat" confident that American elections reflect the will of voters. In March 2022, however, just 44% were confident the country holds free and fair elections, while 56% said they have little or no confidence in American elections.

American politics have been mired in endless controversy during the Trump era, much of which has been inaccurate and hyperbolic. But this problem—that Americans are losing trust in the outcome of elections—is very real and very fundamental. Donald Trump's campaign to undermine the American electoral process, if successful, wouldn't just damage the American body politic; it would weaken the entire Western world of democratic nations. Trust in elections is an essential precondition to democracy.

NOVEMBER 15, 2021
COUNTING VOTES

COUNTING votes in presidential elections can't be done with precision.

First, getting millions of people to vote on the same question will always involve some amount of human error and fraudulent misconduct. Presidential elections are too large and complex to be perfect. Second, election laws will always require line-drawing that advantages one side or the other. That's inherent in rules governing any dynamic, zero-sum system. And third, courts will always have to resolve election disputes. Not every issue can be foreseen and addressed before the votes are cast.

These are facts. They've always been true. And they're not going to change.

There have, moreover, been fundamental electoral deficiencies throughout American history. Slave-owning states got an additional three-fifths of a vote for each slave in their territory. Women gained the franchise merely 100 years ago. John F. Kennedy may have won the 1960 presidential election because of shenanigans by Chicago Mayor Richard J. Daley. (No one knows for sure.) And George W. Bush beat Al Gore in 2000 by a few votes in Florida based on a highly controversial opinion from conservative Supreme Court justices.

So what, then, has kept American democracy moving forward despite its myriad election problems? The good faith and sound judgment of candidates and election officials.

Despite being well aware of elections' inherent imperfections, these key participants have sustained public confidence in the franchise. State officials have largely done exemplary work counting votes. And candidates on the losing side of close elections have recognized that conceding defeat is part of the fuel that keeps the engine of democracy moving forward.

Indeed, is there any doubt that Al Gore genuinely thought he won the 2000 presidential election? No. The former vice president nonetheless conceded defeat after the Supreme Court spoke—not as an endorsement of the Court's decision but as part of his obligation to American democracy. "Let there be no doubt, while I *strongly* disagree with the court's decision, I accept it," Gore said in his concession speech. "I accept the finality of this outcome which will be ratified next Monday in the Electoral College. And tonight, for the sake of our unity as a people and the strength of our democracy, I offer my concession."

That's how it has always worked: Losing candidates have conceded—for the sake of American democracy—even if they strongly believed they actually won.

Until now.

Now, Donald Trump is the loser. And he possesses neither good faith nor sound judgment.

Trump is continuing on with the "Big Lie," the delusion that he (not Joe Biden) was the real winner of the 2020 presidential election. He is asserting one false allegation after another. In an October 27, 2021 letter to the editors of the *Wall Street Journal*, for example, Trump made the following baseless claims (among many others) about the election in Pennsylvania:

- "305,874 voters were removed from the rolls after the election on Nov. 3rd."
- there were "57,000 duplicate registrations."
- there were "39,911 people who were added to voter rolls while under 17 years of age."
- "17,000 mail-in ballots [were] sent to addresses outside of Pennsylvania."

The *Wall Street Journal's* editors appropriately called these claims "bananas."

Yet the Republican Party is going along with it. In droves. The leading Republican in the House of Representatives, Kevin McCarthy, is a Trump ally. In a Politico and Morning Consult poll released last week sixty percent of Republicans said the 2020 presidential election results should definitely or probably be overturned.

And, worst of all, Trump is positioning pro-Trump ideologues to be in charge of states' presidential-election operations in 2024. As Rick Hasen, co-director of the Fair Elections and Free Speech Center at the University of California, Irvine, told CNN: "It is incredibly dangerous to support people for office who do not accept the legitimacy of the 2020 election. It suggests that they might be willing to bend or break the rules when it comes to running elections and counting votes in the future."

Trump has identified the most critical election vulnerability of all: the people who count the votes. It has been the good faith and sound judgment of these people— like Georgia Secretary of State Brad Raffensperger, who rejected Trump's pressure to reverse Georgia's 2020 election results—that has sustained America's election integrity and, therefore, its democratic legitimacy.

Trump is maneuvering the pieces to checkmate American democracy. In plain view. He has captured the hearts and minds of tens of millions of Americans. If he also captures the pens of those who tally the votes, an essential pillar of American democracy—free and fair elections—will hang in the balance.

DECEMBER 15, 2021
DON'T LET THE JANUARY 6 INVESTIGATION
DISTRACT FROM WHAT WE ALREADY KNOW

THE Congressional investigation into the January 6, 2021 riot at the United States Capitol is generating lots of fanfare. And understandably so. The riot was a disturbing low point in American history. Recent headlines highlight Steve Bannon's indictment for refusing to cooperate with investigators and former Department of Justice lawyer Jeffrey Clark's plans to plead the fifth amendment during his upcoming testimony.

But the pursuit of additional information about January 6 shouldn't detract from or obscure what we already know. This is not a situation—like the Mueller investigation—where there is some ambiguous smoke and we need an investigation to determine whether there is fire.

When it comes to the events surrounding January 6, we are already choking on smoke as the fire blazes before us.

Indeed, what we already know constitutes an unprecedented offense to American democracy. We already know, for example, that before the election Donald Trump spent months undermining the election's integrity. On May 26, 2020, for example, Trump tweeted that "[t]here is NO WAY (ZERO!) that Mail-In Ballots will be anything less than substantially fraudulent. Mail boxes will be robbed, ballots will be forged & even illegally printed out & fraudulently signed." On August 24 he asserted that "[t]he only way they can take this election away from us is if this is a rigged election."

And so on.

We already know, moreover, that in the two months after the election—before January 6—Trump doubled down on his baseless claims: "He only won in the eyes of the FAKE NEWS MEDIA," Trump tweeted about Joe Biden. "I concede NOTHING! We have a long way to go. This was a RIGGED ELECTION!"

We already know that, during this time, Trump didn't just tell lies. He tried to coerce the Georgia Secretary of State to commit election fraud. He and Jeffrey Clark tried to capture the Department of Justice after Attorney General William Barr—who flatly rejected Trump's claims of election fraud—left office. He initiated baseless litigation in numerous courts. He pressured Vice President Mike Pence to overturn the results. And, of course, he helped to plan and organize the January 6 rally itself.

We already know that on January 6 Trump held the infamous rally and directed his supporters to the Capitol. He again publicly pressured Pence to overturn the election results. And he openly supported the rioters—while they roamed the Capitol hallways looking for Pence—in a Twitter video.

And, finally, we already know that Trump is carrying on with his open assault on America's electoral system. Trump's baseless accusations of election fraud continue.

The January 6 Committee should, of course, continue on with its important investigative work. And there are undoubtedly critical facts that have yet to emerge.

But while the Committee wrestles with the nuances of Bannon's assertion of executive privilege and Clark's pleading the fifth, it's essential for Americans not to focus disproportionately on these sideline skirmishes. We must see clearly what's already right in front of our faces. We already know that the sitting president of the United States spent months feverishly trying to stage a coup from the Oval Office. And, no matter what we learn from here, how we respond to this affront to American democracy will fundamentally shape our nation going forward.

JANUARY 18, 2022
THE GOOD NEWS ABOUT BAD FAITH

America's political discourse is growing more toxic by the day. Donald Trump won't stop accusing Democrats of stealing the 2020 presidential election. Former Republican Speaker of the House Newt Gingrich accused Republican Congresswoman Liz Cheney of being a criminal for investigating the January 6, 2021 riot at the United States Capitol. And, generally, each side of the political aisle thinks the other is merely a rabid pack of bad actors.

Indeed, Americans just can't stop accusing each other of bad faith.

Take *Washington Post* columnist Greg Sargent's claim that Sen. Joe Machin's "inflation fearmongering" about the Build Back Better Act "is saturated in bad faith." According to Sargent, the West Virginia Democrat "has reportedly been presented with reams of counter-evidence, which he ignores."

And then there's Iowa Senator Joni Ernst, who said President Biden made bad-faith statements about America's exit from Afghanistan. According to Ernst, a Republican, "President Biden's bad faith spin of his catastrophic exit and gross mishandling of the deteriorating situation in Afghanistan is insulting."

These are strong allegations. But are they true? And, generally, is the amount of bad faith in politics really as high as it seems?

Sure, there's undoubtedly *some* bad faith in politics. Even if ten percent of Congress operates in bad faith, for example, that's over 50 politicians. But there's more confusion and misunderstanding in politics than there is bad faith—a lot more.

What's actually happening, more than anything, is the prevalence of what University of Toronto psychology professor Keith Stanovich calls myside bias. This bias "occurs when people evaluate evidence, generate evidence, and test hypotheses in a manner biased toward their own prior opinions and attitudes."

Myside bias causes people to embrace and amplify what fits their preexisting beliefs and to diminish and ignore what doesn't. It's a powerful filter that fundamentally alters how people perceive reality. As a result, two people with opposing worldviews will see two very different worlds—just like two musicians with different sheets of music will play two very different songs.

Of course, most people understand there's bias and partisanship in politics. But several important things aren't well understood. The first is that myside bias is powerful and widespread—it's not simply quirky misunderstandings at the margins. According to Harvard professor Steven Pinker, myside bias is "probably the most powerful of all the cognitive biases."

Nor does myside bias only impact one side of the political aisle and not the other. Myside bias fundamentally distorts how most Americans view politics. As Stanovich explains, liberals and conservatives alike "accept and reject science depending upon whether the conclusion aligns with the political policy that maps their ideological position."

Myside bias, moreover, is just as pervasive among intelligent and informed people as among others. As Stanovich has written, "Research across a wide variety of myside bias paradigms has revealed a somewhat surprising finding regarding individual differences. The magnitude of the myside bias shows very little relation to intelligence."

Yale professor Dan Kahan has shown, in fact, that intelligent and informed people are often the most biased of all. "The capacities associated with science literacy," Kahan explains, "can actually impede public recognition of the best available evidence and deepen pernicious forms of cultural polarization."

Myside bias thus not only makes people, of all stripes, think their group is good, but also—mistakenly—that the other group is bad. Or, as Pinker puts it, myside bias makes us think "that our own tribe is virtuous and wise and knowledgeable and the other tribe is evil and stupid and ignorant."

Indeed, was Manchin, as Sargent alleges, really operating in bad faith by expressing concern about Build Back Better's impact on inflation? Probably not. While the economics can be debated, many people—on both sides of the political aisle—have concerns about rising inflation.

Likewise, is it really true, as Ernst asserts, that Biden's statements about Afghanistan were made in bad faith? This is doubtful. All human beings, including the President of the United States, tend to view their own decisions in a favorable light. Would Ernst levy the same charge against former Vice President Dick Cheney, who in 2015 *still* believed invading Iraq in 2003 was the right decision?

The good news is that bad faith is much less prevalent than it seems. People tend to be decent and well-intentioned. The bad news, however, is that misunderstanding rooted in myside bias is ubiquitous. And the accusers, like Sargent and Ernst, are usually just as afflicted as everyone else.

FEBRUARY 18, 2022
DON'T GENERALIZE ABOUT THE JANUARY 6 PROTESTORS

Most people learn early on the dangers of generalizing. English poet William Blake put it bluntly several hundred years ago: "To generalize is to be an idiot."

For some reason the lesson doesn't stick. America's political discourse is overflowing with multifaceted categories that few bother to unpack. Case in point: the January 6 protesters.

This is not a monolithic group. There are at least three separate categories of January 6 protestors. One is the violent rioters who stormed the United States Capitol. They are insurrectionists and criminals who should be prosecuted to the fullest extent of the law. (And if any politicians—including Donald Trump—facilitated the violence, they, too, should be prosecuted.)

Another category is those who stayed outside the Capitol and non-violently protested what they believe was a fraudulent 2020 presidential election. These people are mistaken (some even delusional), but they are not criminals. Impassioned non-violent protest—however misinformed or misguided—is a core tradition of American democracy.

And a third category is those who went to the January 6 Trump rally on the Ellipse and then went home. They didn't even go to the Capitol.

A striking example of the failure to recognize these distinctions made headlines recently when the Republican National

Committee censured Representatives Liz Cheney (R. Wyo.) and Adam Kinzinger (R. Ill.), the two Republican members of the congressional January 6 committee. According to the RNC, "Representatives Cheney and Kinzinger are participating in a Democrat-led persecution of ordinary citizens engaged in legitimate political discourse ...."

Huh? Legitimate political discourse? What?

This statement makes no distinction, whatsoever, between the peaceful rally-goer who merely attended the Trump rally and the violent, trespassing insurrectionist who assaulted police officers within the halls of the Capitol. Was the RNC really saying everyone subject to the January 6 committee's sweeping investigation engaged in legitimate political discourse, even those with blood on their hands?

Apparently so.

Generalizations like this are all too common. And the ambiguity doesn't just cause confusion. It poisons the debate. The RNC's critics took the statement literally and accused Republicans of endorsing deadly violence. As the *New York Times* put it: "The Republican Party on Friday officially declared the Jan. 6, 2021, attack on the Capitol and events that led to it 'legitimate political discourse'...."

Despite RNC Chair Ronna McDaniel's meager efforts to walk things back on Twitter, the censure's text hasn't changed. And many Americans now think the Republican party itself stands for political violence and deadly insurrection. That's not good for anyone.

This state of affairs is the predictable result of the RNC's extraordinarily sloppy failure to draw any distinctions between the January 6 protesters—a heterogeneous group whose activities ranged from non-violent (and, yes, legitimate) political discourse all the way to violent insurrection.

William Blake would not be impressed.

AUGUST 8, 2022
MOBILIZING THE MOB

THE FBI's search of Donald Trump's Mar-a-Lago estate angered many Republicans. Kansas Senator Josh Hawley, for example, called the FBI's actions "an unprecedented assault on democratic norms and the rule of law."

According to Trump, the search exemplifies America's free-falling descent under the Biden administration. "These are dark times for our Nation," he warned.

Yet this story is just beginning. The former president's rhetoric is bound to escalate dramatically as the FBI's investigation unfolds. At a Texas rally in January, Trump brazenly threatened prosecutors investigating him in various jurisdictions. "If these radical, vicious, racist prosecutors do anything wrong or corrupt," he said, "we are going to have in this country the biggest protests we have ever had."

Trump is thus actively organizing an alternative to legitimate government power—a large, violent mob mobilized to intimidate government officials and thwart their objectives. Sound familiar? The January 6, 2021 mob of Trump insurrectionists that stormed the United States Capitol may have been merely a precursor to something bigger and more consequential.

This threat goes to the core of American democracy. The government's monopoly on the use of force is, indeed, an essential precondition to civilized society. As political scientist Ezra Suleiman wrote in his book, Dismantling Democratic States, when a government loses its monopoly on force, it ceases being a state, and "its form of organization becomes indistinguishable from other types of organization." And as Joshua Horwitz and Casey Anderson put it in Guns, Democracy, and the Insurrectionist Idea, a "state must be able to enforce its judicial or administrative rulings: if it is outgunned by individuals or factions, it is not functioning as a democratic state (in fact, it is not functioning as a state at all) and is reverting to a pregovernmental society where might makes right and political equality is at best an abstract ideal."

This is exactly what Trump has been threatening—to use a violent faction to outgun prosecutors investigating his conduct.

And it might just work. Prosecutors have vast discretion to decide whether or not to pursue a matter and nothing requires them to bring a case, even if crimes have clearly been committed. In this instance, fear of large-scale violence could be the difference between initiating proceedings and declining to prosecute.

Indeed, whether to prosecute Trump will inevitably be a close call. On the one hand, the government has probable cause to believe that Trump violated the law. The FBI's Mar-a-Lago search warrant would not otherwise have been approved by a federal judge. On the other, seeking a guilty verdict from a jury—which must be unanimous—in a country where Trump has historically high approval ratings among Republicans is a bold objective. No prosecutor wants to lose to Trump in court.

Concerns about the reactions of Trump's millions of supporters will weigh heavily in the Department of Justice's analysis. Trump knows this. And he knows how to whip his supporters into a frenzy of anger and violence. The violent rhetoric has, indeed, already begun. In a pro-Trump online forum one person posted: "I'm just going to say it. Garland needs to be assassinated. Simple as that." Another person posted: "kill all feds."

We don't know, yet, the detailed basis for the FBI's Mar-a-Lago search. Nor do we know the intentions behind the government's initiative. If this is an attempt to keep Trump from running in 2024 it may be foolhardy as nothing in the Constitution prevents someone with a criminal record from assuming the presidency. We do know, however, that the search feeds the long-held narrative among many Trump supporters that the federal government (the "Deep State") is unfairly targeting their chosen leader.

On January 6, 2021, Trump organized a mob to try and physically prevent the orderly transfer of executive power. We should expect him to mount a similar initiative regarding his intensifying criminal investigations. The rule of law in America—already teetering on the ragged edge of a breakdown—hangs in the balance.

CONCLUSION

THIS book begins with my favorite quote about government, from Abraham Lincoln: "There are few things wholly evil or wholly good. Almost everything, especially of government policy, is an inseparable compound of the two, so that our best judgment of the preponderance between them is continually demanded."

My worldview, and, thus, the columns in this book, reflect this truth: that nothing big and complicated is entirely good or bad, but rather a fluid and ever-shifting balance between the two. Smart people say stupid things. Bad people do good things. Good ideas breed bad results. And so on. As Barack Obama put it: "The world is messy; there are ambiguities. People who do really good stuff have flaws. People who you are fighting may love their kids, and share certain things with you."

So what, then, is the current preponderance of good and bad in the large, ambiguous, multi-faceted American polity?

The answer lies in the people. The key to any democracy is the people themselves. As Franklin D. Roosevelt said, "Let us never forget that government is ourselves and not an alien power over us. The ultimate rulers of our democracy are not a President and senators and congressmen and government officials, but the voters of this country."

Indeed, the strength of the essential principles of American government corresponds tightly with the rationality and responsibility of the American people. It always will. And while America withstood the Trump presidency—and its core governmental institutions remain strong—it is, on balance, a more dysfunctional nation than before Trump took office.

And it's getting worse, not better. Tens of millions of Trump supporters refuse to accept the 2020 presidential-election results. Many won't wear masks or take Covid-19 vaccinations. Demagogues run for office with increasing frequency. Elected officials regularly throw seething partisan tantrums from the seat of government. The two political parties speak different languages, and show little interest in finding an interpreter. And partisan-driven false narratives pound the airwaves and fill the headlines.

The American people are growing more unmoored from reality and American democracy can't help but follow. While America has reached new heights of scientific and technical achievement, it has also descended to new lows of irrationality and political toxicity. "Human rationality is very much in the news," Harvard professor Steven Pinker noted recently, "as we struggle to understand how an era with unpreceded scientific sophistication could harbor so much fake news, conspiracy theorizing, and 'post-truth' rhetoric." This irrationality is no longer at the fringes of American society: it has reached the highest levels of power in the world's most influential nation. The longer this goes on the more the fabric of American democracy frays. The farther America deviates from the mean the more difficult it will be to revert back. In June of 2022 the January 6 committee in Congress unearthed new evidence of Trump supporters' disturbing efforts to overturn the 2020 presidential election and the Supreme Court shocked the system by gratuitously overturning *Roe v. Wade*. And, at the center of the storm, remains Donald Trump, the foremost threat to American democracy and, still, the most powerful Republican in the country—by a wide margin.

The American stress test continues.

ACKNOWLEDGMENTS

I'D first like to thank Amira Ghanim and Todd Swift at Black Spring Press Group in London, UK. This book would not have been possible without their wise guidance and steadfast support. Heartfelt thanks as well to my classmates and professors in law school who helped spark my passion for constitutional law. I am grateful, moreover, to the many people who have been patient enough over the years to listen to my views on American democracy, and generous enough to share their own.

Finally, I would like to thank the publications who welcomed me onto their platforms and published the initial versions of the columns in this book. Among them: *The New York Daily News, San Francisco Chronicle, Baltimore Sun, Chicago Sun-Times, Jerusalem Post, Yahoo News, Palm Beach Post, Sun Sentinel, Hamilton Spectator, Orlando Sentinel, St. Louis Post-Dispatch, Holland Sentinel, Patriot News, Sierra Sun, Buffalo News, Union, Arizona Daily Star, Detroit News, Salt Lake Tribune, Columbus Dispatch, Star Courier, Standard Examiner, City Paper Bogotá, Inforum, Asbury Park Press, Tennessean, Chattanooga Times Free Press, Boulder Daily Camera, Creston News Advertiser, Carthage News, Capital Journal, Watertown Public Opinion, Pocono Record, Deming Headlight, Modern Ghana, Williston Herald, Anchorage Press, Skiatook Journal, Huntsville Item, News-Register, Longview News-Journal, Arizona Capitol Times, Fergus Falls Journal, Daily Nation, Herald-Dispatch, Iowa State Daily, National Herald, Garden Island, Colorado Springs Gazette, Longview Daily*

News, MinnPost, Muskokan, Flamborough Review, National Newswatch, Medium, Crossville Chronicle, Tucson Weekly, Boulder Weekly, New Rockford Transcript, Tillamook Headlight Herald, Lowveld Post, Fayetteville Observer, London Bulletin, Caledon Enterprise, Vaal Today, Voice of Vienna, Polk County Itemizer-Observer, Dalhousie Gazette, Monroe News, Bedford Now, Laramie Boomerang, and *Aspen Daily News.*